The Ghetto, and Other Poems

The Ghetto, and Other Poems

An Annotated Edition

Lola Ridge

edited and with an Introduction by
Lawrence Kramer

Fordham University Press   New York   2023

Fordham University Press has no responsibility for the persistence or accuracy of
URLs for external or third-party Internet websites referred to in this publication
and does not guarantee that any content on such websites is, or will remain,
accurate or appropriate.

Fordham University Press also publishes its books in a variety of electronic formats.
Some content that appears in print may not be available in electronic books.

Visit us online at www.fordhampress.com.

Library of Congress Cataloging-in-Publication Data available online at https://
catalog.loc.gov.

25 24 23   5 4 3 2 1

First edition

FIGURE 1. Lola Ridge. Undated studio photograph. Courtesy of the Sophia Smith Collection of Women's History, Lola Ridge Papers (smith_ssc_ms00131_as337510 _ 001), Smith College Special Collections.

Contents

FIGURE 2. Hester Street ca. 1903. U.S. National Archives.

Introduction

I. Lola Ridge and *The Ghetto*

Born in Dublin in 1873, Rose Emily Ridge reinvented herself as Lola Ridge in 1907. The new name marked her arrival in a new place. She had come to San Francisco via New Zealand, where she grew up as an immigrant in a hardscrabble mining town, and Australia, where she began publishing poems and studied art at the Acadamie Julienne in Sydney. After arriving in America she presented herself as ten years younger than she was (a fiction she would maintain until her death) and pursued a career in both art and literature. In 1908 she left her only child, a son, in a Los Angeles orphanage and moved to New York City, settling in Greenwich Village. In New York she worked as an advertising copywriter, an illustrator, a factory hand, and an artist's model. Committed all her life to radical causes, above all to the American labor movement, she also went to work for the anarchist philosopher Emma Goldman and the birth control pioneer Margaret Sanger. By the 1920s, her editorial work for two leading modernist journals, *Others* and *Broom*, made her a key part of a literary set populated by figures who would later become canonical American modernists: William Carlos Williams, Marianne Moore, Jean Toomer, and Hart Crane. Ridge's name is not yet on this list. The present critical edition of her 1918 volume, *The Ghetto, and Other Poems*, is meant to suggest that it should be.

The title poem is a panoramic depiction of Jewish life on the Lower East Side of Manhattan. *The New Republic* published an abbreviated version (reprinted here in the appendix) in April 1918. When B. W. Huebsch published the complete text in *The Ghetto, and Other Poems* in September, the result was a literary sensation. The poet Alfred Kreymbourg, in a *Poetry Magazine* review, praised the "The Ghetto" for its "sheer passion, deadly accuracy of versatile images, beauty, richness, and incisiveness of epithet, unfolding of adventures, portraiture of emotion and thought, pageantry of pushcarts—the whole lifting, falling, stumbling, mounting to a broad, symphonic rhythm" (Kreymbourg 1919, 337). Louis Untermeyer, writing in the *New York Evening Post* (today's *New York Post*), found "The Ghetto" "at once personal in its piercing sympathy and epical in its sweep. It is studded with images that are surprising and yet never strained or irrelevant; it glows with a color that is barbaric, exotic, and as local as Grand Street" (Untermeyer 1919, sec. 3, p. 1).

Each of Ridge's subsequent four books of poetry moved in a new direction; her passion for reinventing herself never flagged, though her sympathy with workers and the poor runs throughout like a leitmotif. *Sun-Up* (1920) centers on an extended semiautobiographical account of a troubled girlhood; *Red Flag* (1927) is full of political protest and revolutionary fervor; *Firehead* (1930) is a book-length account of the Crucifixion; *Dance of Fire* (1935) mixed political poems with—talk about reinvention!—a long mystical series of sonnets, "Via Ignis." These books were generally well received, but none of them approached *The Ghetto* in its impact. Even so, Ridge won several poetry prizes during the 1930s. At her death in 1941, the *New York Times* obituary characterized her as one of America's leading poets. And then she more or less disappeared for seventy-five years.

The reasons for this fall from grace are plain enough. Ridge's sex obviously played a role, as did her uncompromising left-wing politics; that the title poem of her third book, *Red Flag*, is a paean to the Russian Revolution did not help, especially once the Cold War had begun and, not long after, Joseph McCarthy's political reign of terror. Moreover, Ridge's best-known poems were social realist texts, as much documentaries as they were fictions. They drew their readers into the messy reality that the poetry favored by the postwar literary establishment was supposed to transcend. Ridge could not have made a better case for her own obscurity if she had tried.

In a favorable review of *The Ghetto* volume, Hart Crane identified the key impediment. The title poem, he wrote, "is like a miniature *Comedie humaine*, with the dominant note of sadness that runs through Balzac's narratives so insistently." This certainly reads as a compliment, but with a scruple that Crane quickly develops. Nineteenth-century novels may have been rooted in social observation; twentieth-century poetry could not stop with that, as Crane's, for example, pointedly would not. The aesthetic of poetry demanded a symbolic apparatus. But because Ridge's poetry is so "vivid," Crane makes an exception for her:

> I have spoken more of the social significance of Miss Ridge's work than strictly aesthetic canons would probably admit, because I have felt the interpretive aspects of her work to be its most brilliant facet. When work is so widely and minutely reflective of its time, then, certainly, other than questions of pure *aesthetique* must be considered. (Crane 1966, 202)

But it might be argued that the real problem here is the opposition of social significance and aesthetic design, even though Crane bends it in Ridge's favor. The opposition was and is widely maintained. Aesthetic canons demand that the fact be redeemed by the symbol. But does social concern necessarily preclude symbolic articulation? Why? Can one even convey social concern *without* symbolic articulation? The question, perhaps, is not whether the symbolic apparatus is there; it is always there. The question is how well it works.

That question each reader of "The Ghetto" and *The Ghetto* will answer individually. But to do so requires making the apparatus visible, which is one aim of the volume in hand. "The Ghetto" does not hide its symbolic underpinnings, but neither does it advertise them. The poem seems to suggest that any empathetic observer of life on New York's Lower East Side is already immersed in a universe of signs. The material reality of the place is saturated with import, as the Brooklyn Bridge would be in Crane's *The Bridge* (1930). Crane, in any case, might—should—have thought more about a short poem he read so often that his copy of *The Ghetto* (preserved in his papers at Columbia University) falls open to it. The poem anticipates both the title and the presiding symbol of his own magnum opus:

To Brooklyn Bridge

Pythoness body—arching
Over the night like an ecstasy—
I feel your coils tightening . . .
And the world's lessening breath.

But then, as Crane's bête noir T. S. Eliot once remarked, great poets never borrow. They steal.

Crane engages in unacknowledged dialogue with *The Ghetto* throughout *The Bridge*. The coils of Ridge's Brooklyn Bridge, arching over the night, return in the lines that frame "Atlantis," Crane's concluding nocturne: "Through the bound cable strands, the arching path / Upwards" and "One arc synoptic of all tides below" (Crane 2011, 127, 134). Ridge singles out the Woolworth Building among Manhattan's skyscrapers in "Manhattan"; Crane does the same in "Virginia." Ridge depicts a resurgent sexuality amid the Lower Manhattan cityscape in "The Ghetto"; Crane does likewise in "The Harbor Dawn." Ridge figuratively connects the flow of life in the Ghetto to the River Jordan; Crane makes the symbolic crossing of the East River (underground, via the subway) the cardinal moment of transition in "The Tunnel" and in *The Bridge* overall. The point of noting these connections is not to question Crane's "originality" but to mark the pertinence of Ridge as one of his interlocutors.

Recent years have seen a few notable efforts to win a new audience for Ridge. Bonnie Kime Scott's 2007 anthology, *Gender in Modernism*, reprints selections from "The Ghetto," which it describes as "the first feminist poem about ghetto life published in America, and probably the first poem about ghetto life in general published in English" (96). Daniel Tobin published a selection of Ridge's early works in 2007 and a complete collection of them through *Red Flag* in 2018. (The later work has not inspired much interest; there seems to be an informal consensus that Ridge's major achievement is *The Ghetto*, especially "The Ghetto.") Carolyn Maun's 2012 *Mosaic of Fire* situates Ridge in a circle of friendships among modernist women writers. Cary Nelson's chapter on New York modernism in the 2015 *Cambridge Companion to Modern American Poetry* reads Ridge in the teens and twenties as part of the literary scene in Greenwich Village alongside Edna St. Vincent Millay and e.e. cummings (Kalaidjian 2015, 50–64). Terese Svoboda published a comprehensive biography, *Anything That Burns You: A Portrait of Lola Ridge, Radical Poet*, in 2016; the title phrase is Ridge's reply to the question of what poets should be writing about in 1925. Svoboda has also written numerous articles on Ridge that can be found online; partly as a result, Ridge has developed a fairly robust presence on the internet, as a Google search will quickly show (Derby 2009; Pinsky 2011; Rumens 2018; Simonds 2020). There is also an archive of Ridge's papers, including correspondence, letters, artwork, diaries, and memorabilia, available in the Smith College Library. Lola Ridge has not yet received her due, but she is no longer just a footnote in the saga of American modernism.

The present volume does not recover a fugitive original; the bare text of *The Ghetto, and Other Poems* is readily available both in print and online. Instead, this edition provides the reader with annotations that identify, in one convenient place, the literary and historical details necessary to understand the text—and its symbolic apparatus—fully.

II. An Overview of the Text

The Ghetto divides into three large segments, each disposed toward a characteristic type of poetry, a genre of its own. The first is a panoramic account of life in Manhattan, with emphasis on the immigrant experience on the one hand and the excesses of capitalist plutocracy on the other. "The Ghetto" is the paramount example; hence its pride of place in the volume. It is followed by a series of city poems grouped under the rubric "Manhattan Lights" and ranging in topic from the arrogance of the skyscrapers to the miseries of the Bowery. The second segment, "Labor," is just what its title declares, a portrait of the American labor movement and its travails. The two most ambitious poems in the group are "The Song of Iron," which takes up a prophetic, quasi-biblical stance on behalf of exploited workers, and "Frank Little at Calvary," an account of the 1917 murder of a prominent labor leader in Butte, Montana. The final segment is "Accidentals," primarily consisting of personal lyrics, many of them deliberately enigmatic; in these poems the symbolic element dominates, sometimes to the point of willful obscurity—another trait that Hart Crane must have found congenial. The title "Accidentals" suggests the miscellaneous character of this segment, but it is also, I suspect, meant in its musical sense, referring to notes marked to fall outside the key signature of a score. The poetry is wayward; it will not play nice. "Nice," Ridge once remarked, "is the one adjective in the world that is laughable applied to any single thing I have ever written" (Svoboda 2016b).

Many of the poems in *The Ghetto* are impressive, but the volume stands or falls on the strength of "The Ghetto," so I will concentrate my further remarks on that signature text.

"The Ghetto" is perhaps best read with, and against, another portrait of the era's Jewish life in Lower Manhattan, this one written by a very canonical author, Henry James. In the summer of 1904, James returned from his home in England for a yearlong visit to the United States. In 1907 he published a record of his travels, *The American Scene*. Although the book cuts a wide swath along the Eastern seaboard and through the South (where James, among other things, tried to reckon with the legacies of slavery), its true center is New York, James's boyhood home. The modern city struck him as "terrible," in part because of its physical transformation and in part because of who had come to live there.

Henry James had not been in the United States since 1884. He therefore had no opportunity to witness the massive waves of European immigration, especially of Italians and Jews, that had occurred in the interim via the port of New York. When he returned, he had trouble recognizing the place he had left. He felt, even against his better judgment, and despite the fact that he could speak only as an expatriate, that the country he thought of as his, or that had been his in his youth, had been opened too much to "the foreign," "the alien." The sense of dispossession weighed heavily on him despite his own perfectly clear awareness that his attitude was unreasonable:

> Who and what is an alien, when it comes to that, in a country peopled from the first . . . by migrations at once extremely recent, perfectly traceable and urgently required? They are still, it would appear, urgently required—if we look about far enough for the urgency; though of that truth such a scene as New York may well make one doubt. Which is the American, by these scant measures?—which is *not* the alien, over a large part of the country at least, and where does one put a finger on the dividing line? (James 1993, 459)

The Ghetto fascinates James as much as it distresses him, and he tries to sustain a fair-minded ambivalence toward it—and he fails. He looks on helplessly as a familiar old order is progressively displaced by an alien modern confusion. He finds the chaos most fully exemplified in two contrary forms, both centered in Manhattan: the skyscrapers rising over the city and the Jews rising up in the Ghetto--the Lower East Side. He is particularly struck by the sheer density of the Jewish population, especially its children:

> The children swarmed above all—here was multiplication with a vengeance; and the number of very old persons, of either sex, was almost equally remarkable; the very old persons being in equal vague occupation of the doorstep, pavement, curbstone, gutter, roadway, and every one alike using the street for overflow. As overflow, in the whole quarter, is the main fact of life—I was to learn later on that, with the exception of some shy corner of Asia, no district in the world known to the statistician has so many inhabitants to the yard—the scene hummed with the human presence beyond any I had ever faced. (James 1993, 464–65)

James understood the Ghetto as the scene of a foreign "conquest"; it turned New York into the "city of redemption" that reversed the Jewish diaspora. The Ghetto was the New Jerusalem. James was not an inveterate anti-Semite, but he simply could not recognize that the people he felt to be so "foreign" in language and culture were doing the exactly the same thing in America as he had spent his life doing in Italy and England. Or rather, he does recognize it but fails to follow through on its implications. James (referring to himself in the third person) describes riding on a streetcar—"a foreign carful":

> The great fact about his companions was that, foreign as they might be, newly inducted as they might be, they were *at home*, really more at home, at the end of their few weeks or months or their year or two, than they had ever in their lives been before; and that *he* was at home too, quite with the same intensity: and yet that it was this very equality of condition that, from side to side, made the whole medium so strange. (James 1993, 460; original emphasis)

James's difficulties were compounded by the sheer multiplication of "foreign" ethnic categories that persisted in the United States well into the twentieth century. The hyphenated American did not yet exist, not in 1906 and not in 1918. National origin, or the national origin of one's ancestors, had almost the potency and almost the invidiousness of racial classification, with which it sometimes overlapped. This state of affairs was epitomized in New York in the Independence Day parade of 1918, a gargantuan ten-hour affair designed to demonstrate the loyalty of the various ethnicities to the nation and to its role in World War I. On July 5 the *New York Times* printed an extensive account of the "pageant," detailing the contribution of each national group (there were more than forty of them; "Foreign Born in Line" read a subhead). The Jews came just after the Italians and the Irish:

> The Jewish section had . . . been reduced to 10,000 from 50,000 applicants. . . . [M]ore than fifty cantors marched in a body, and a float showed Judea enthroned and joining hands with the Allies. Another float represented Judas Maccabeus and his warriors fighting for liberty . . . while still another represented Haym Solomon raising funds for Washington's Army.[1]

James, it seems safe to say, would have been appalled. Ridge would have felt right at home. She would, of course, have scorned the coercive patriotism, but she might have been pleased that, according to the *Times*, the Jewish segment of the parade concluded with representatives from "scores of labor unions."

Ridge's perspective is James's in reverse. She too takes the skyscrapers, the overflowing streets, and the culture of the Ghetto as key markers of national transformation. She too, like so many others then and now, sees the force of transformation as a conflict between modernity and tradition. She even takes note of those overabundant children: "Baskets full of babies / Like grapes on a vine." Ridge's chief difference from James, her sympathies aside, is that she portrays this conflict as internal to the Ghetto community. The Ghetto is not in conflict with America; America is in conflict with itself within the Ghetto. For Ridge, becoming American means becoming Americanized. The immigrant generation in the Ghetto represents the Old World; its children belong to the new, even if they are not welcomed by it. (They are already taking

---

1. The full article is available from the online archive of the *Times*: www.nytimes.com/1918/07/05/archives/daylong-pageant-pictures-america-united-for-war-parade-sweeping.html. Haym Solomon (1740–85) was one of the principal financial backers of the American Revolution.

non-Jews as lovers.) Unlike James's, Ridge's Ghetto is not a social monolith. It is a riven heterogeneity, exactly like the city and the nation that houses it.

This heterogeneity is the key to the symbolic dimension of "The Ghetto." The poem progresses as a sequence of nine scenes, some linked to others, some independent; in form it is half a documentary record, half a modernist collage. Until its final segment, its aim is not to make sense of life in the Ghetto but to portray the efforts of those who live there to make sense of it. Amid the hubbub and hardship, making sense is even more important than making a living. Accordingly, the panoramic sweep of the text repeatedly narrows down to the labor and desire of individuals, one of whom, Sadie Sodos, comes close to being the narrator's alter ego. These individual efforts to make meaning inevitably fall short, but they do not stop coming. For the elders, the efforts tend to rely on the preservation of Jewish tradition or Jewish law; for the young, they veer toward sexual freedom and radical politics.

Meanwhile the poem also incorporates moments that question the very notion of making sense, in particular of reconciling an outmoded heritage with an inexorable but uncertain future. These moments generally turn on a mysterious encounter or observation. Symbolic articulation arrests the flow of the text with a promise of fuller knowledge, but it conceals as much as it reveals. The cardinal instance is perhaps the narrator's chance meeting, in the street, with a small girl to whom she gives an orange. Her effort to connect with the child, whose "eyes have the glow / Of darkened lights," is doomed from the start, for more reasons than one (the episode, in segment III, is extended), but its failure condenses metaphorically into a breakdown of language: the girl speaks only Yiddish and the narrator only English. Unlike Sadie, the lost girl resists the narrator's empathy; she is merely puzzled by the gift; she runs away abruptly, an alter ego that might have been but will not be. The narrator subsequently surmises that the girl is haunted by the memory of persecution, but it is not clear whether the memory is hers, her parents', or the Ghetto's, and in any case the reader has no way of knowing whether the narrator is right.

In this context the concluding section of the poem is either a breakthrough or a breakdown. Again, readers will decide for themselves. The segment pivots by taking the life of the Ghetto as a manifestation of Life at large. The hubbub becomes vibrancy, or so the narrator wants (us) to believe:

Life!

> Startling, vigorous life,
> That squirms under my touch,
> And baffles me when I try to examine it. . .
> Life,
> Articulate, shrill,
> Screaming in provocative assertion,
> Or out of the black and clotted gutters.

Is "Life" just the name for something that the narrator, that Ridge (for she always speaks for herself, even in fictions), can apprehend but not comprehend, or is it a moralizing term that substitutes for that elusive comprehension? However one responds, Ridge avoids submitting the Life she discovers in the Ghetto to rule or category; it metamorphoses further with every attempt to fix it. And in that respect it is the right note on which to end, since this protean disposition is precisely that of the Ghetto itself. Where James regrettably saw something like a giant fish tank, "some vast sallow aquarium in which innumerable fish, of over-developed proboscis, were to bump together, for ever, amid heaped spoils of the sea" (1993, 464), Ridge finds a collective body without boundaries—what Gilles Deleuze and Felix Guattari call a body without organs:

> Pent, overflowing
> Stoops and façades,
> Jostling, pushing, contriving,
> Seething. . .

But Ridge's aesthetic—and, Hart Crane notwithstanding, she has one— demands that this ever-shifting plural body must continually incarnate itself in the singular: the fugitive child, a red-bearded man with a ruined face, the light in Sadie's window, and many more, up Hester Street, down Grand.

III. *The Ghetto* and American Modernism

American modernist poetry was anything but triumphant in its own day. It flourished primarily in little magazines with small circulations, among them the two that Ridge worked for in the twenties. Book publication was hard for modernist poets; William Carlos Williams, for example, had to pay for the publication of his *Al Que Quiere!* in 1917 and *Sour Grapes* in 1921. The dominant mode in the early twentieth century was still the genteel lyric: formally timid, elevated in tone, sententious, and above all determined to avoid entanglement in historical time. A good measure of the situation can be gleaned from Harriet Monroe's *Poetry Magazine*, which was hospitable to both genteel tradition and modernist invention. The issue for September 1918, chosen because *The Ghetto, and Other Poems* was published in the same month, is revealing. I do not have the space to be more than synoptic here, but the magazine's online archive makes it easy to read the contents in full.[2]

Of the thirteen poets published in the issue, only one, Robert Gilbert Walsh, refers to the everyday conditions of modern urban life. Walsh is also exceptional in acknowledging the presence of what James called "the alien" in American society:

> Sometimes the gaunt old man
> Who teaches Latin and Greek in High School
> Sits in Weinberg's Café
> On rainy nights.
> ("The Djinn")

This modest reference is a far cry from what one can find in *Al Que Quiere!* ("Are not these Jews and—Ethiopians? / The world is young, surely! Young / and colored like—a girl that has come upon / a lover! Will that do?" [47]) let alone *The Ghetto*, but it is something.

The issue's opening poem, "The Empire of China Is Crumbling Down," by Vachel Lindsay, is a faux-historical fable coupling imperial China with Arthurian romance, much of it in the form of rhymed couplets or quatrains.

---

2. www.poetryfoundation.org/poetrymagazine/issue/70401/september-1919.

(Lindsay does manage to squeeze in one passing reference to Napoleon.) Modern history appears only in Mary Willis Shuey's "Quilts," a lyric concerning a quilt passed down from the speaker's great-aunt, whose lover had "gone / To fight with the South" in the Civil War. The rest of the issue dwells in a kind of poetic Neverland, a kingdom of Nature and Beauty, sometimes evoked with a modest formal freedom, sometimes bound into stanza forms. Few of the poems, even those obviously influenced by the Imagist ideal of pointed sensuous detail, can resist pointing morals. All tacitly assume a homogeneous readership, which is to say a white one; the category at the time would have excluded not only Blacks but also Jews and Italians. (Of course the full list is much longer.) There is also a tacit agreement that sex is off limits as a topic. Here is a short sampler:

> O grass, flowers, trees unfruitful,
>   Caught while your sun was high,
> Buried deep in the sand-dune's keep,
>   Is all of life gone by?
> Can a springing bough lift your glory now
>   And give it back to the sky?
> ("Sand-Dunes," Janet Norris Bangs)

> Love is the heart's last light to die!
>   Though one should strive in stubborn pain
> To quench its beauty utterly,
>   Yet were his labor vain.
> ("Though One Should Strive," Nancy Byrd Turner)

> I burn
> With all the beauty
> That I have known
> And have dreamed of
> Under the quivering fountains
> Of light flowing
> From the radiant sun.
> ("Driftwood Burning," Zoé Akins)

Climbing desperately toward the heights
I glance in terror behind me,
To be deafened—to be shattered
By a thunderbolt of beauty.
("Mountain Trails," Marjorie Allen Seiffert)

For Ridge and the poets of her circle, what needed to be shattered was verse like this, partly for aesthetic reasons but mainly because they thought it embodied a lie. The lie was the denial of history, or more exactly the evasion of history in the present and the history *of* the present, history as a force that sweeps through the lives, the work, the bodies, the loves, and the material conditions of people in the real world, in real time.

"The Ghetto" meticulously details how each of these areas of experience looks and feels in its chosen cityscape. It does so by gradually broadening its perspective beyond Sadie Sodos and her family to take in the other residents of the Ghetto, many of whom receive sharp character sketches as the poem works its way toward the culminating panorama of Life. Each change of focus demands its own set of minute particulars. The men who sit in a "dingy café" are old, like Walsh's Latin teacher, but Ridge, unlike Walsh, describes the café in detail and tells us that the old men are "muffled in woollens." The sensory observation (full of muffled sounds) not only implies that the heat in the café is inadequate but also, with the double meaning of "muffled," intimates the historical predicament of the old men. Unlike their children, these half-mummified figures are tethered to the world they left behind. The world they have come to has smothered their power of self-expression and reduced the shape of their bodies to vague outlines.

The subsequent "Manhattan Lights" section of *The Ghetto* continues the broadening beyond the confines of Hester Street. "Spring" describes an unexpectedly fresh day on the Bowery that dispels the fetid air and allows for moments of pleasure mixed with incredulity. One child, akin to the mysterious girl of "The Ghetto," forgets that she is poor and malnourished, but the smile that her pleasure brings to her mother's face is self-canceling:

People sniff the air with an upward look—
Even the mite of a girl
Who never plays . . .

Her mother smiles at her
With eyes like vacant lots
Rimming vistas of mean streets
And endless washing days . . .

It is hard not to hear in these lines an echo of the conclusion to T. S. Eliot's "Preludes," published in 1917: "The worlds revolve like ancient women / Gathering fuel in vacant lots" (Eliot 1963, 15).

The lines also exemplify a feature of Ridge's poetic voice that is basic to the New York segments of *The Ghetto* and especially to the title poem. Ridge writes as neither a participant nor an observer but as a wavering commingling of the two. Here she observes the tiny girl looking upward and the mother smiling, but she also slides imperceptibly from seeing the mother's eyes to seeing *with* those eyes into streets that are also the alleys of memory. The compound voice assumes wider political and historical resonance in "The Ghetto," where it breaks down the difference between Jews like Sadie and non-Jews like Ridge and persists even when the difference inevitably revives, as in the encounter with the Yiddish-speaking child. Ridge does not speak for the Ghetto but invites the Ghetto to speak through her.

The compound voice is even fluid in its sex. It is never other than a woman's voice, in particular the voice of a woman who refuses the romantic abstractions and sexual reticence of her counterparts in that September 1918 issue of *Poetry*. But in the highly erotic eighth section of "The Ghetto," the poem's climax in every sense of the term, the voice speaks as explicitly and intimately about men's sexual feelings as it does about women's. Ridge's voice respects no boundaries. Yet this same voice remains distinctly, even defiantly, historical. It does not want to be "universal," but it refuses the authority of categories and the tyranny of fixed distinctions.

IV. Modernism and the City

The vein of modernism tapped by "The Ghetto" and "Manhattan Lights" depended on a conception of the modern city as something not merely new, but unprecedented. The city marked a break with the past in matter as well as in mind. The break was radical and irrevocable. Overcrowded with people, traffic, machines, commerce, labor, wealth, poverty, misery, revelry, sex, and sensation, the city was the scene where history would, and should, be remade. It demanded recognition; it demanded testimony; it demanded protest. For American writers in the early twentieth century, the twin paradigms of this city were New York and Chicago. Unlike the London and Dublin of the two most famous texts of urban modernism, T. S. Eliot's "The Waste Land" and James Joyce's *Ulysses*, the cities of American modernism in the teens and twenties neither missed nor mythified the past; they just left it behind. (Crane's *The Bridge* and Williams's *Paterson* [1946–58] would later turn back to the paradigm set by Eliot and Joyce.)

"The Ghetto" and "Manhattan Lights" share their approach to the city with Carl Sandburg's *Chicago Poems* (1916) and John Dos Passos's novel *Manhattan Transfer* (1925). Ridge's "Manhattan Lights" come above all—literally so—from skyscrapers. Here is Sandburg on the subject:

> Toward the end of the afternoon all work slackens and
> all jobs go slower as the people feel day closing on
> them.
> One by one the floors are emptied. . . The uniformed
> elevator men are gone. Pails clang. . . Scrubbers
> work, talking in foreign tongues. Broom and water
> and mop clean from the floors human dust and spit,
> and machine grime of the day.
> Spelled in electric fire on the roof are words telling
> miles of houses and people where to buy a thing for
> money. The sign speaks till midnight. ("Skyscrapers")

And here is Dos Passos:

> Jobless, Jimmy Herf came out of the Pulitzer Building. He stood
> beside a pile of pink newspapers on the curb, taking deep breaths,
> looking up the glistening shaft of the Woolworth. . . . . He turned north
> and began to walk uptown. As he got away from it the Woolworth
> pulled out like a telescope. He walked north through the city of shiny
> windows, through the city of scrambled alphabets, through the city of
> gilt letter signs. (*Manhattan Transfer*, 379)

And Ridge:

> Diaphanous gold,
> Veiling the Woolworth
> Rising slender and stark
> Mellifluous-shrill as a vender's cry,
> And towers squatting graven and cold
> On the velvet bales of the dark.
> ("Manhattan")

But the primary source of American urban modernism is Walt Whitman. *Leaves of Grass* is full of passages celebrating the multiplicity and vitality of the city (Whitman 2002). Many of them employ Whitman's signature technique of stringing details together without further connection. (Carried to extremes, this rhetorical device, formally known as parataxis or asyndeton, becomes the measure of an existential condition.) The American urban modernists follow suit, though with celebration more a goal than a given. But Whitman could do that too.

> The blab of the pave, tires of carts, sluff of boot-soles, talk of the
> promenaders,
> The heavy omnibus, the driver with his interrogating thumb, the
> clank of the shod horses on the granite floor,
> The snow-sleighs, clinking, shouted jokes, pelts of snow-balls,
> The hurrahs for popular favorites, the fury of rous'd mobs,
> The flap of the curtain'd litter, a sick man inside borne to the
> hospital. . .
> What groans of over-fed or half-starv'd who fall sunstruck or in
> fits,
> What exclamations of women taken suddenly who hurry home
> and give birth to babes,
> What living and buried speech is always vibrating here, what
> howls restrain'd by decorum,
> Arrests of criminals, slights, adulterous offers made, acceptances,
> rejections with convex lips,

I mind them or the show or resonance of them—I come and I
    depart.
        ("Song of Myself," lines 154–66, *Leaves of Grass*, 32)

The phrase closing that last quotation, "I come and I depart," points to a par-
ticular feature of Whitman's urban poetry that is perhaps even more important
for Ridge than the general panoramic impetus. Whitman likes to present him-
self as a wandering passerby arrested by the things he sees or hears; "Give me
the streets of Manhattan!" he writes; "Give me Broadway . . . / People, endless,
streaming, with strong voices, passions, pageants, / Manhattan streets with
their powerful throbs."[3] Whitman the city dweller is Whitman the *flâneur*.

Flâneurie, or strolling, became an image of modernity in nineteenth-cen-
tury Paris. The *flâneur* was a man of leisure who wandered amid urban
crowds as a detached observer. The twentieth-century thinker Walter Ben-
jamin took a particular interest in this figure. He focused particularly on
Charles Baudelaire, whose *Fleurs du Mal* (Flowers of Evil, 1857) turned urban
rambling into the source of poetry. Baudelaire's *flâneur* persona was ironic,
even in empathy, where Whitman's was entranced, but the two shared, to
steal a phrase from Eliot, "such a vision of the street / As the street hardly
understands" ("Preludes" III, in Eliot 1963, 15).

In an article aptly titled "Electric Currents of Life" (the phrase comes from
the poem) the critic Nancy Berke describes the narrator of "The Ghetto" as
an immigrant *flaneuse*—a pointedly female stroller who lays unprecedented
claim to the freedom of the city streets: "In 'The Ghetto,' Ridge attempts
to recast *flâneurie* for the twentieth-century world in which women become
urban walkers. 'Mothers waddle in and out' and daughters express a 'free
camaraderie' on the ghetto streets" (2010, 39). The poem as a whole incor-
porates a pageant of women engaged in work, politics, sex, commerce, and
motherhood; "the community fabric," writes Berke, "is a 'motley weave'
threaded together by women" (38). Ridge's *flaneuse* persona shares both the

3. "Give Me the Splendid Silent Sun," lines 27–28, 36–37, *Leaves of Grass*, 263. See
also "Mannahatta," *Leaves of Grass*, 397, which incidentally celebrates "Immigrants
arriving, fifteen or twenty thousand in a week" (line 12). Whitman's most sustained
depiction of urban wandering is "Crossing Brooklyn Ferry," in which the "strolling"
takes place on shipboard between Brooklyn and Manhattan.

entrancement and the empathy of Whitman's *flâneur,* but empathy is its hallmark. The Ghetto, home to the most stigmatized of immigrant groups in early twentieth-century America, called for that empathy with a force rivaled for Ridge only by the call of labor—ultimately just the same call. At the same time the Ghetto, a city within the iconic modern city, stood as the decisive testing ground for the claim that life could withstand the machine of modernity and perhaps even manage to flourish.

V. The Sound of Life

Ridge's New York Ghetto remains Henry James's "city of redemption" but not in the sense that James intended. The Ghetto does not redeem "Israel," the Jewish diaspora. It redeems, instead, the very history whose all-pervasive force the Ghetto epitomizes. Paradoxically, however, if not surprisingly, this redemption is itself a historical process, and forever incomplete. The generational conflict between tradition and modernity, Talmudic and secular Judaism, that plays out on the Lower East Side is part of it. Writing "The Ghetto" is part of it. Linking the sweatshops of the Ghetto to the iron foundries of Pittsburgh is part of it too. Even Ridge's culminating mantra of "LIFE!" is more historical than it is biological. When Ridge says that Life runs through the Ghetto in "electric currents," her phrase not only recalls Walt Whitman's "body electric" but also refers to the electrification of the modern city. The currents pass through the jingle of coins and pushcarts and through arguments in meeting rooms and "Roumanian wine-shops" and "little Russian tea-rooms,"

> Making unknown circuits,
> Or out of spent particles stirring
> Feeble contortions in old faiths
> Passing before the new.

Another part of the process is the sound it produces. The Ghetto reverberates. Its sound is not an incidental background but a defining condition. The language of "The Ghetto" is mostly speechlike rather than sonorous; in that respect Ridge's affinity among her peers is with Williams, not with Crane. But the poem nonetheless invokes a distinctive soundscape, an echo chamber of innumerable human voices overlapping and colliding, "Majestic discordances / Greater than harmonies," ranging from curses to cries of ecstasy, all mixed with the sound of bells and sewing machines, animal cries and the creaking of old furniture. The life of the Ghetto is a polyphony and a cacophony at once.

Perhaps it was this auditory sensitivity—if I may close on a personal note—that first drew my attention to "The Ghetto." I'm a composer as well as a scholar, and in 2018 I was looking for a text to set to music for the "Migrations" Festival that Carnegie Hall was sponsoring the following March. My search led to a passage in Ridge's poem that deals with nocturnal sounds; having found it, I read the whole text with equal absorption. Only later did I realize that the poem had jogged the memory of a real soundscape, actually two of them, from my early childhood. My father at one time owned a lunch counter in North Philadelphia, a Black ghetto, and his father worked in the rag trade, selling clothes in a Jewish ghetto in West Philadelphia. This was when I was very young, and my memory of these places is vague and scanty. But one thing I can recall from both is the wave on wave of voices unlike mine that more than anything, for me, defined the atmosphere of each: puzzling, enveloping, exciting. Ridge, to my ear, captured this kind of sonic environment better than any comparable poet—just one more reason to bring her neglected work to your attention here.

The Ghetto, and Other Poems

FIGURE 3. Hester Street ca. 1898. Wikimedia Commons.

The Ghetto

To the American People

Will you feast with me, American People?
But what have I that shall seem good to you!

On my board are bitter apples
And honey served on thorns,
And in my flagons fluid iron,[1]
Hot from the crucibles.

How should such fare entice you!

1. The flagons and apples allude to the Song of Solomon 2:5: "Stay me with flagons, comfort me with apples: for I am sick of love." (Biblical quotations, with a single exception, are drawn from the King James Version.)

The Ghetto

I

Cool, inaccessible air
Is floating in velvety blackness shot with steel-blue lights,
But no breath stirs the heat
Leaning its ponderous bulk upon the Ghetto
And most on Hester Street . . .

The heat . . .
Nosing in the body's overflow,
Like a beast pressing its great steaming belly close,
Covering all avenues of air . . .

The heat in Hester Street,
Heaped like a dray
With the garbage of the world.

Bodies dangle from the fire escapes
Or sprawl over the stoops . . .
Upturned faces glimmer pallidly—
Herring-yellow faces, spotted as with a mold,
And moist faces of girls
Like dank white lilies,
And infants' faces with open parched mouths that suck at the air
    as at empty teats.

Young women pass in groups,
Converging to the forums and meeting halls,
Surging indomitable, slow
Through the gross underbrush of heat.
Their heads are uncovered to the stars,[2]
And they call to the young men and to one another
With a free camaraderie.
Only their eyes are ancient and alone . . .

The street crawls undulant,

Like a river addled
With its hot tide of flesh
That ever thickens.
Heavy surges of flesh
Break over the pavements,[3]
Clavering like a surf—[4]
Flesh of this abiding
Brood of those ancient mothers who saw the dawn break over Egypt . . .
And turned their cakes upon the dry hot stones[5]

2. By leaving their heads uncovered, the young women flaunt their status as unmarried (see note 9, below).

3. The descriptions of Hester Street in this and the preceding segment are not exaggerated. Henry James's statement (quoted in the introduction) that in 1905 New York's Lower East Side was the most densely populated region in the Western world was true, or close to it. Period photographs bear out the point; people on the streets of the Ghetto were commonly packed shoulder to shoulder, hemmed in by pushcarts on all sides. James recalls that his visit, on a summer evening, left him with the sense of "a great swarming, a swarming that had begun to thicken, infinitely, as soon as we had crossed to the East side and long before we had got to Rutgers Street" (James 1993, 464).

4. *Claver* is a primarily Scottish verb meaning to prattle, chatter, or gossip. "Clavering like a surf" seems to suggest that the tide-like motion of bodies constantly jostling each other ("heavy surges of flesh") is audible as well as tangible.

5. Making matzo (unleavened bread). The reference is to Exodus 12:39: "And they baked unleavened cakes of the dough which they had brought out of Egypt; for it

And went on
Till the gold of the Egyptians fell down off their arms . . .[6]
Fasting and athirst . . .
And yet on . . .

Did they vision—with those eyes darkly clear,
That looked the sun in the face and were not blinded—
Across the centuries
The march of their enduring flesh?
Did they hear—
Under the molten silence
Of the desert like a stopped wheel—[7]
(And the scorpions tick-ticking on the sand . . .)
The infinite procession of those feet?

II

I room at Sodos'[8]—in the little green room that was Bennie's—
With Sadie
And her old father and her mother,
Who is not so old and wears her own hair.[9]

---

was not leavened, because they were driven out of Egypt and could not wait, nor had they prepared provisions for themselves."

6. See Exodus 3:22: "Every woman shall ask her neighbor and any woman staying in her house for silver and gold jewelry and clothing, and you will put them on your sons and daughters. So you will plunder the Egyptians" (New KJV).

7. Exodus 14:24–25: "And it came to pass, that in the morning watch the LORD looked unto the host of the Egyptians through the pillar of fire and of the cloud, and troubled the host of the Egyptians, And took off their chariot wheels, that they drave them heavily: so that the Egyptians said, Let us flee from the face of Israel; for the LORD fighteth for them against the Egyptians."

8. The surname is Polish; together with the old man's trade, it suggests that the family had emigrated from a shtetl, exchanging a rural ghetto (subject to the pogroms described in section III) for an urban one.

9. The wig, usually black with extended bangs, worn by Orthodox married women to meet the requirement that they cover their hair for modesty. Sadie's mother stands in contrast to the "little old woman" of section V.

Old Sodos no longer makes saddles.
He has forgotten how.
He has forgotten most things—even Bennie who stays away
    and sends wine on holidays—
And he does not like Sadie's mother
Who hides God's candles,[10]
Nor Sadie
Whose young pagan breath puts out the light—
That should burn always,
Like Aaron's before the Lord.[11]

Time spins like a crazy dial in his brain,
And night by night
I see the love-gesture of his arm
In its green-greasy coat-sleeve
Circling the Book,
And the candles gleaming starkly
On the blotched-paper whiteness of his face,
Like a miswritten psalm . . .
Night by night
I hear his lifted praise,
Like a broken whinnying
Before the Lord's shut gate.[12]

Sadie dresses in black.
She has black-wet hair full of cold lights

10. And therefore does not observe the Sabbath, also unlike the old woman in section V.

11. The name "Aaron" means "light-bringer." See Numbers 8:2–3: "Speak unto Aaron, and say unto him, When thou lightest the lamps, the seven lamps shall give light over against the candlestick. And Aaron did so; he lighted the lamps thereof over against the candlestick, as the LORD commanded Moses."

12. "Shut gate." See Psalms 24:7: "Lift up your heads, O ye gates; and be ye lifted up, ye everlasting doors; and the King of glory shall come in."

And a fine-drawn face, too white.
All day the power machines
Drone in her ears . . .[13]

All day the fine dust flies
Till throats are parched and itch
And the heat—like a kept corpse—[14]
Fouls to the last corner.

Then—when needles move more slowly on the cloth
And sweaty fingers slacken
And hair falls in damp wisps over the eyes—
Sped by some power within,
Sadie quivers like a rod . . .
A thin black piston flying,
One with her machine.

She—who stabs the piece-work with her bitter eye
And bids the girls: "Slow down—
You'll have him cutting us again!"
She—fiery static atom,
Held in place by the fierce pressure all about—
Speeds up the driven wheels

13. Sewing machines. Sadie works in a sweatshop, where she would have earned somewhere between $5 and $12 (between $78 and $188 in 2021 dollars) per fifty-two-hour week. Typically on upper stories, these working floors for seamstresses were crowded and poorly ventilated—hence the fine dust and heat in the next few lines. Ridge would have assumed that her readers were familiar with the catastrophic fire at the nearby Triangle Shirtwaist factory, which in 1911 had killed 146 garment workers, 123 of them women, most of them Jewish or Italian immigrants between the ages of fourteen and twenty-three. The fire was the worst industrial disaster in the city's history, notorious in part because locked doors, meant to keep workers from taking furtive breaks, made escape impossible.

14. "Kept corpse": in contravention of Jewish law, which requires burial within twenty-four hours of death.

And biting steel—that twice
Has nipped her to the bone.

Nights, she reads
Those books that have most unset thought,
New-poured and malleable,
To which her thought
Leaps fusing at white heat,
Or spits her fire out in some dim manger of a hall,
Or at a protest meeting on the Square,
Her lit eyes kindling the mob . . .
Or dances madly at a festival.
Each dawn finds her a little whiter,
Though up and keyed to the long day,
Alert, yet weary . . . like a bird
That all night long has beat about a light.

The Gentile lover, that she charms and shrews,
Is one more pebble in the pack
For Sadie's mother,
Who greets him with her narrowed eyes
That hold some welcome back.
"What's to be done?" she'll say,
"When Sadie wants she takes . . .
Better than Bennie with his Christian woman . . .
A man is not so like,
If they should fight,
To call her Jew . . ."

Yet when she lies in bed
And the soft babble of their talk comes to her
And the silences . . .
I know she never sleeps

Till the keen draught blowing up the empty hall
Edges through her transom
And she hears his foot on the first stairs.

Sarah and Anna live on the floor above.
Sarah is swarthy and ill-dressed.
Life for her has no ritual.
She would break an ideal like an egg for the winged thing at the core.
Her mind is hard and brilliant and cutting like an acetylene torch.
If any impurities drift there, they must be burnt up as in a clear flame.
It is droll that she should work in a pants factory.
—Yet where else . . . tousled and collar awry at her olive throat.
Besides her hands are unkempt.
With English . . . and everything . . . there is so little time.
She reads without bias—
Doubting clamorously—
Psychology, plays, science, philosophies—
Those giant flowers that have bloomed and withered, scattering their
     seed . . .
—And out of this young forcing soil what growth may come—
     what amazing blossomings.

Anna is different.
One is always aware of Anna, and the young men turn their heads
     to look at her.
She has the appeal of a folk-song
And her cheap clothes are always in rhythm.
When the strike was on she gave half her pay.
She would give anything—save the praise that is hers
And the love of her lyric body.

But Sarah's desire covets nothing apart.
She would share all things . . .

Even her lover.

III

The sturdy Ghetto children
March by the parade,[15]
Waving their toy flags,
Prancing to the bugles—
Lusty, unafraid . . .
Shaking little fire sticks
At the night—
The old blinking night—
Swerving out of the way,
Wrapped in her darkness like a shawl.

But a small girl
Cowers apart.
Her braided head,
Shiny as a black-bird's
In the gleam of the torch-light,
Is poised as for flight.
Her eyes have the glow
Of darkened lights.

She stammers in Yiddish,
But I do not understand,
And there flits across her face

15. Probably a parade organized by the Socialist Party on behalf of workers' rights. Such parades were frequent events in Lower Manhattan in the early years of the century, especially during midsummer; they continued during the war years. The details mentioned by Ridge are typical: milling crowds, music, torchlight, flags (sometimes American, sometimes red), and the participation of children. One Jewish observer of a strike-related parade in 1910, Abraham Rosenberg, wrote, "In my mind I could only picture to myself such a scene taking place when the Jews were led out of Egypt" (Leinenweber 1977, 155).

A shadow
As of a drawn blind.
I give her an orange,
Large and golden,
And she looks at it blankly.
I take her little cold hand and try to draw her to me,
But she is stiff . . .
Like a doll . . .

Suddenly she darts through the crowd
Like a little white panic
Blown along the night—
Away from the terror of oncoming feet . . .
And drums rattling like curses in red roaring mouths . . .
And torches spluttering silver fire
And lights that nose out hiding-places . . .
To the night—
Squatting like a hunchback
Under the curved stoop—
The old mammy-night[16]
That has outlived beauty and knows the ways of fear—
The night—wide-opening crooked and comforting arms,
Hiding her as in a voluminous skirt.

The sturdy Ghetto children
March by the parade,
Waving their toy flags,
Prancing to the bugles,
Lusty, unafraid.
But I see a white frock

16. "Mammy": common Irish usage, unconnected to the demeaning term applied
to African American women.

And eyes like hooded lights
Out of the shadow of pogroms
Watching . . . watching . . .

IV
Calicoes and furs,
Pocket-books and scarfs,
Razor strops and knives
(Patterns in check . . .)

Olive hands and russet head,
Pickles red and coppery,
Green pickles, brown pickles,
(Patterns in tapestry . . .)

Coral beads, blue beads,
Beads of pearl and amber,
Gewgaws, beauty pins—
Bijoutry for chits—
Darting rays of violet,
Amethyst and jade . . .
All the colors out to play,
Jumbled iridescently . . .
(Patterns in stained glass
Shivered into bits!)

Nooses of gay ribbon
Tugging at one's sleeve,
Dainty little garters
Hanging out their sign . . .
Here a pout of frilly things—
There a sonsy[17] feather . . .

17. "Sonsy": Comely, plump, busty.

(White beards, black beards
Like knots in the weave . . .)[18]

And ah, the little babies—
Shiny black-eyed babies—
(Half a million pink toes
Wriggling altogether.)
Baskets full of babies
Like grapes on a vine.

Mothers waddling in and out,
Making all things right—
Picking up the slipped threads
In Grand Street at night—
Street like a great bazaar,
Crowded like a float,
Bulging like a crazy quilt
Stretched on a line.[19]

18. Verse paragraphs 1–4. In its short lines and strong rhythms, this catalog of flashy items meant to tempt the unwary buyer carries an ironic echo Christina Rossetti's *Goblin Market* (1862):

"Rare pears and greengages,
Damsons and bilberries,
Taste them and try:
Currants and gooseberries,
Bright-fire-like barberries,
Figs to fill your mouth,
Citrons from the South,
Sweet to tongue and sound to eye,
Come buy, come buy."
(Rossetti 1865, 2, lines 23–31)

19. Grand Street was the commercial center of the Jewish Lower East Side, with intersecting streets housing pushcart markets (at Mott and Orchard Streets), outdoor jewelry markets (on the Bowery), and bed linen markets (on Allen Street).

But nearer seen
This litter of the East
Takes on a garbled majesty.

The herded stalls
In dissolute array . . .
The glitter and the jumbled finery
And strangely juxtaposed
Cans, paper, rags
And colors decomposing,
Faded like old hair,
With flashes of barbaric hues
And eyes of mystery . . .
Flung
Like an ancient tapestry of motley weave
Upon the open wall of this new land.

Here, a tawny-headed girl . . .
Lemons in a greenish broth
And a huge earthen bowl
By a bronzed merchant
With a tall black lamb's wool cap upon his head . . .
He has no glance for her.
His thrifty eyes
Bend—glittering, intent
Their hoarded looks
Upon his merchandise,
As though it were some splendid cloth
Or sumptuous raiment
Stitched in gold and red . . .

He seldom talks
Save of the goods he spreads—

The meager cotton with its dismal flower—
But with his skinny hands
That hover like two hawks
Above some luscious meat,
He fingers lovingly each calico,
As though it were a gorgeous shawl,
Or costly vesture
Wrought in silken thread,
Or strange bright carpet
Made for sandaled feet . . .

Here an old grey scholar stands.
His brooding eyes—
That hold long vistas without end
Of caravans and trees and roads,
And cities dwindling in remembrance—
Bend mostly on his tapes and thread.

What if they tweak his beard—
These raw young seed of Israel
Who have no backward vision in their eyes—
And mock him as he sways
Above the sunken arches of his feet—
They find no peg to hang their taunts upon.
His soul is like a rock
That bears a front worn smooth
By the coarse friction of the sea,
And, unperturbed, he keeps his bitter peace.

What if a rigid arm and stuffed blue shape,
Backed by a nickel star[20]

20. "Nickel star": a policeman's badge, worn by the portly figure stuffing the blue
uniform.

Does prod him on,
Taking his proud patience for humility . . .
All gutters are as one
To that old race that has been thrust
From off the curbstones of the world . . .
And he smiles with the pale irony
Of one who holds
The wisdom of the Talmud stored away
In his mind's lavender.

But this young trader,
Born to trade as to a caul,[21]
Peddles the notions of the hour.
The gestures of the craft are his
And all the lore
As when to hold, withdraw, persuade, advance . . .
And be it gum or flags,
Or clean-all or the newest thing in tags,
Demand goes to him as the bee to flower.
And he—appraising
All who come and go
With his amazing
Sleight-of-mind and glance
And nimble thought
And nature balanced like the scales at nought—
Looks Westward where the trade-lights glow,[22]
And sees his vision rise—
A tape-ruled vision,

21. In folklore to be born under a caul is a sign of good luck.
22. "Westward": toward the skyscrapers on Manhattan's West Side but also in the direction taken by immigrants coming from Europe to the United States and by the nation's expansion across the continent.

Circumscribed in stone—[23]
Some fifty stories to the skies.[24]

V
As I sit in my little fifth-floor room—[25]
Bare,
Save for bed and chair,
And coppery stains
Left by seeping rains
On the low ceiling
And green plaster walls,
Where when night falls
Golden lady-bugs

23. The stone of the "circumscribed" office towers—written on all sides, with a possible play on "circumcised"—replaces the tables of the Law. Ridge's slide into reflexive anti-Semitism in a poem otherwise strenuously opposed to it may have its roots in Karl Marx's toxic essay "On the Jewish Question" (1843): "What is the worldly religion of the Jew? *Huckstering.* [Compare Ridge's "sleight-of-mind."] What is his worldly God? *Money.* Very well then! Emancipation from huckstering and money, consequently from practical, real Judaism, would be the self-emancipation of our time . . . . If the Jew recognizes that this *practical* nature of his is futile and works to abolish it, he extricates himself from his previous development and works for *human emancipation* as such and turns against the supreme practical expression of human self-estrangement" (Marx 2009; original emphasis).

24. Manhattan's skyscrapers, still relatively new in 1918, were explicitly represented as temples of commerce. Writing in 1905, Henry James called them "mercenary monsters" and deplored their "multiplied mass of floors and windows," which, he continued, "were going to bring in money—and was not money the only thing a self-respecting structure could be thought of as bringing in?" (James 1993, 434–35). The details in this passage—a stone building west of Grand Street "some fifty stories" high—identifies the object of the trader's gaze as the fifty-three-story Woolworth Building, then just five years old. Ridge returns to the image in "Manhattan"; see note 2, below.

25. The narrator's room; but soon after arriving in New York, Ridge herself lived in a five-by-seven room in a Lower East Side tenement (Svoboda 2016a, 101). The dimensions suggest what is known as a "dumbbell" tenement, which admitted light and air only via an air shaft between adjacent buildings.

Come out of their holes,
And roaches, sepia-brown, consort . . .[26]
I hear bells pealing
Out of the gray church at Rutgers Street,[27]
Holding its high-flung cross above the Ghetto,
And, one floor down across the court,
The parrot screaming:
Vorwärts . . . Vorwärts . . .[28]

The parrot frowsy-white,
Everlastingly swinging
On its iron bar.

A little old woman,
With a wig of smooth black hair
Gummed about her shrunken brows,
Comes sometimes on the fire escape.
An old stooped mother,
The left shoulder low
With that uneven droopiness that women know
Who have suckled many young . . .
Yet I have seen no other than the parrot there.

I watch her mornings as she shakes her rugs
Feebly, with futile reach
And fingers without clutch.

26. Like the crowding on Hester Street, this detail is not exaggerated. Svoboda (2016a, 100) records that "roaches were stacked inches high in the apartments photographed by Lewis Hine" at the turn of the century.

27. "Gray church": the Catholic Church of St. Theresa (originally Rutgers Presbyterian). The "high-flung cross" sits atop the clock tower.

28. *Vorwärts*: German for "Forward!" used in the imperative. As *Forverts*, Yiddish for "forward" and the name of the progressive Yiddish-language newspaper, *Forward*, originally published on the Lower East Side.

Her thews are slack
And curved the ruined back
And flesh empurpled like old meat,
Yet each conspires
To feed those guttering fires
With which her eyes are quick.

On Friday nights
Her candles signal
Infinite fine rays
To other windows,
Coupling other lights,
Linking the tenements
Like an endless prayer.

She seems less lonely than the bird
That day by day about the dismal house
Screams out his frenzied word . . .
That night by night—
If a dog yelps
Or a cat yawls
Or a sick child whines,
Or a door screaks on its hinges,
Or a man and woman fight—
Sends his cry above the huddled roofs:
Vorwärts . . . Vorwärts . . .

VI
In this dingy cafe
The old men sit muffled in woollens.
Everything is faded, shabby, colorless, old . . .
The chairs, loose-jointed,
Creaking like old bones—

The tables, the waiters, the walls,
Whose mottled plaster
Blends in one tone with the old flesh.

Young life and young thought are alike barred,
And no unheralded noises jolt old nerves,
And old wheezy breaths
Pass around old thoughts, dry as snuff,
And there is no divergence and no friction
Because life is flattened and ground as by many mills.

And it is here the Committee—[29]
Sweet-breathed and smooth of skin
And supple of spine and knee,
With shining unpouched eyes
And the blood, high-powered,
Leaping in flexible arteries—
The insolent, young, enthusiastic, undiscriminating Committee,
Who would placard tombstones
And scatter leaflets even in graves,
Comes trampling with sacrilegious feet!

The old men turn stiffly,
Mumbling to each other.
They are gentle and torpid and busy with eating.
But one lifts a face of clayish pallor,
There is a dull fury in his eyes, like little rusty grates.
He rises slowly,

29. A branch committee of the Socialist Party. The socialist movement grew
exponentially in New York during the first two decades of the twentieth century,
especially among Jewish garment workers. By late 1914, the party had 135 branches
in the city (Leinenweber 1977, 165). Cafés and taverns were common sites for com-
mittee meetings.

Trembling in his many swathings like an awakened mummy,
Ridiculous yet terrible.
—And the Committee flings him a waste glance,
Dropping a leaflet by his plate.
A lone fire flickers in the dusty eyes.
The lips chant inaudibly.
The warped shrunken body straightens like a tree.
And he curses . . .
With uplifted arms and perished fingers,
Claw-like, clutching . . .
So centuries ago
The old men cursed Acosta,[30]
When they, prophetic, heard upon their sepulchres
Those feet that may not halt nor turn aside for ancient things.

VII

Here in this room, bare like a barn,
Egos gesture one to the other—
Naked, unformed, unwinged
Egos out of the shell,
Examining, searching, devouring—
Avid alike for the flower or the dung . . .
(Having no dainty antennae for the touch and withdrawal—
Only the open maw . . .)

Egos cawing,

30. Acosta: Uriel da Costa (1585–1640), Portuguese philosopher who converted to Judaism from Catholicism but was twice excommunicated by rabbinical authorities for writing books (one of which was publicly burned) questioning orthodox doctrines. Given the celebration of "Life" in the poem's concluding section, it is worth noting that da Costa was "cursed" in part for denying the immortality of the soul. Ridge's use of the name "Acosta" suggests that she knew of da Costa through the play *Uriel Acosta* by Karl Gutzkow (1811–78); translated from the German, the play became a mainstay of Yiddish theater.

Expanding in the mean egg . . .
Little squat tailors with unkempt faces,
Pale as lard,
Fur-makers, factory-hands, shop-workers,
News-boys with battling eyes
And bodies yet vibrant with the momentum of long runs,
Here and there a woman . . .

Words, words, words,
Pattering like hail,
Like hail falling without aim . . .
Egos rampant,
Screaming each other down.
One motions perpetually,
Waving arms like overgrowths.
He has burning eyes and a cough
And a thin voice piping
Like a flute among trombones.

One, red-bearded, rearing
A welter of maimed face bashed in from some old wound,
Garbles Max Stirner.[31]
His words knock each other like little wooden blocks.
No one heeds him,
And a lank boy with hair over his eyes
Pounds upon the table.
—He is chairman.

31. Max Stirner (1806–56): post-Hegelian anarchist philosopher. Stirner's mag-
num opus, *The Ego and Its Own* (*Der Einzige und sein Eigentum*, 1845) is radically
anti-authoritarian; the red-bearded man garbles it by understanding the ego in a
merely personal sense. Stirner regarded "egoism" as a state of autonomy achieved in
the final phase of a dialectical process in both persons and societies. No concept can
explain the ego, and no external principle can control it.

Egos yet in the primer,
Hearing world-voices
Chanting grand arias . . .
Majors resonant,
Stunning with sound . . .
Baffling minors
Half-heard like rain on pools . . .
Majestic discordances
Greater than harmonies . . .
—Gleaning out of it all
Passion, bewilderment, pain . . .

Egos yearning with the world-old want in their eyes—
Hurt hot eyes that do not sleep enough . . .
Striving with infinite effort,
Frustrate yet ever pursuing
The great white Liberty,
Trailing her dissolving glory over each hard-won barricade—[32]
Only to fade anew . . .

Egos crying out of unkempt deeps
And waving their dreams like flags—
Multi-colored dreams,
Winged and glorious . . .

A gas jet throws a stunted flame,
Vaguely illumining the groping faces.
And through the uncurtained window

32. "Great white Liberty": not only the Statue but also the bare-breasted figure
of Liberty in Eugene Delacroix's famous painting *Liberty Leading the People* (1830),
linked here to the barricades of the Paris Commune, the radical socialist govern-
ment that ruled Paris from March to May 1871, after the defeat of France in the
Franco-Prussian War.

Falls the waste light of stars,
As cold as wise men's eyes . . .
Indifferent great stars,
Fortuitously glancing
At the secret meeting in this shut-in room,
Bare as a manger.

VIII
Lights go out
And the stark trunks of the factories
Melt into the drawn darkness,
Sheathing like a seamless garment.

And mothers take home their babies,
Waxen and delicately curled,
Like little potted flowers closed under the stars.

Lights go out
And the young men shut their eyes,
But life turns in them . . .

Life in the cramped ova
Tearing and rending asunder its living cells . . .
Wars, arts, discoveries, rebellions, travails, immolations,
        cataclysms, hates . . .
Pent in the shut flesh.
And the young men twist on their beds in languor and dizziness
        unsupportable . . .
Their eyes—heavy and dimmed
With dust of long oblivions in the gray pulp behind—
Staring as through a choked glass.
And they gaze at the moon—throwing off a faint heat—
The moon, blond and burning, creeping to their cots

Softly, as on naked feet . . .
Lolling on the coverlet . . . like a woman offering her white body.

Nude glory of the moon!
That leaps like an athlete on the bosoms of the young girls stripped
    of their linens;
Stroking their breasts that are smooth and cool as mother-of-pearl
Till the nipples tingle and burn as though little lips plucked at them.
They shudder and grow faint.
And their ears are filled as with a delirious rhapsody,
That Life, like a drunken player,
Strikes out of their clear white bodies
As out of ivory keys.

Lights go out . . .
And the great lovers linger in little groups, still passionately debating,
Or one may walk in silence, listening only to the still summons of
    Life—
Life making the great Demand . . .
Calling its new Christs . . .
Till tears come, blurring the stars
That grow tender and comforting like the eyes of comrades;
And the moon rolls behind the Battery
Like a word molten out of the mouth of God.

Lights go out . . .
And colors rush together,
Fusing and floating away . . .
Pale worn gold like the settings of old jewels . . .
Mauves, exquisite, tremulous, and luminous purples
And burning spires in aureoles of light
Like shimmering auras.

They are covering up the pushcarts . . .
Now all have gone save an old man with mirrors—
Little oval mirrors like tiny pools.
He shuffles up a darkened street
And the moon burnishes his mirrors till they shine like phosphorus . . .
The moon like a skull,
Staring out of eyeless sockets at the old men trundling home the
      pushcarts.

IX
A sallow dawn is in the sky
As I enter my little green room.
Sadie's light is still burning . . .
Without, the frail moon
Worn to a silvery tissue,
Throws a faint glamour on the roofs,
And down the shadowy spires
Lights tip-toe out . . .
Softly as when lovers close street doors.

Out of the Battery
A little wind
Stirs idly—as an arm
Trails over a boat's side in dalliance—
Rippling the smooth dead surface of the heat,
And Hester street,
Like a forlorn woman over-born
By many babies at her teats,
Turns on her trampled bed to meet the day.[33]

33. *The New Republic* version of the "The Ghetto" ended with this stanza, without resuming the invocation of Life introduced in section VIII.

LIFE!
Startling, vigorous life,
That squirms under my touch,
And baffles me when I try to examine it,
Or hurls me back without apology.
Leaving my ego ruffled and preening itself.

Life,
Articulate, shrill,
Screaming in provocative assertion,
Or out of the black and clotted gutters,
Piping in silvery thin
Sweet staccato
Of children's laughter,

Or clinging over the pushcarts
Like a litter of tiny bells
Or the jingle of silver coins,
Perpetually changing hands,
Or like the Jordan somberly
Swirling in tumultuous uncharted tides,
Surface-calm.

Electric currents of life,
Throwing off thoughts like sparks,
Glittering, disappearing,
Making unknown circuits,
Or out of spent particles stirring
Feeble contortions in old faiths
Passing before the new.

Long nights argued away
In meeting halls

Back of interminable stairways—
In Roumanian wine-shops
And little Russian tea-rooms . . .

Feet echoing through deserted streets
In the soft darkness before dawn . . .
Brows aching, throbbing, burning—
Life leaping in the shaken flesh
Like flame at an asbestos curtain.

Life—
Pent, overflowing
Stoops and façades,
Jostling, pushing, contriving,
Seething as in a great vat . . .

Bartering, changing, extorting,
Dreaming, debating, aspiring,
Astounding, indestructible
Life of the Ghetto . . .

Strong flux of life,
Like a bitter wine
Out of the bloody stills of the world . . .
Out of the Passion eternal.[34]

34. The concluding reference to Christ's Passion may seem odd in a poem about
a Jewish ghetto. But the specifically Christian meaning of the Passion is actually
revoked here, in keeping with the poem's call for "new Christs" in section VIII and
with the reference to the gray Church of St. Theresa as an intrusive presence in
the Ghetto. Ridge represents the equation of blood and wine as a general historical
condition rather than as the result of a unique act of sacrifice. (She develops the met-
aphor further in the labor poem "Iron Wine," below.) That the wine is bitter perhaps
recalls the bitter herbs of the Passover ceremony, derived from the same condition of
exile and exodus that structures "The Ghetto."

FIGURE 4. Tenement interior. Photograph by Louis Hine. Library of Congress.

Manhattan Lights

FIGURE 5. Woolworth Building (left) and Singer Building (right), 1919.
U.S. Navy National Museum of Naval Aviation.

Manhattan

Out of the night you burn, Manhattan,
In a vesture of gold—
Span of innumerable arcs, [1]
Flaring and multiplying—
Gold at the uttermost circles fading
Into the tenderest hint of jade,
Or fusing in tremulous twilight blues,
Robing the far-flung offices,
Scintillant-storied, forking flame,
Or soaring to luminous amethyst
Over the steeples aureoled—

Diaphanous gold,
Veiling the Woolworth,[2] argently

1. "Arcs": arc lamps (lit by a current sparked between paired electrodes), which replaced gaslights and were replaced by incandescent lights in the illumination of cities. By 1913 arc lamps had been installed throughout most of Manhattan. Their light was very bright and their lampposts accordingly tall, producing the glittering arrays described by Ridge, who uses the image eight times (Landmarks Preservation Commission 1997, 5).

2. The Woolworth Building at 233 Broadway, constructed by Cass Gilbert in 1913 for F. W. Woolworth, founder of an extensive chain of "five-and-ten-cent" stores; in 1918 it was the tallest building in the world. "Vesture of gold . . . Diaphanous gold": the coffered (indented) ceiling of the building's rear lobby is gilded. Both the lobby as a whole and the facade (of limestone and terra-cotta) are lavishly decorated and richly colored.

Rising slender and stark
Mellifluous-shrill as a vender's cry,
And towers squatting graven and cold
On the velvet bales of the dark,
And the Singer's appraising
Indolent idol's eye,[3]
And night like a purple cloth unrolled—

Nebulous gold
Throwing an ephemeral glory about life's vanishing points,
Wherein you burn . . .
You of unknown voltage
Whirling on your axis . . .
Scrawling vermillion signatures
Over the night's velvet hoarding . . .
Insolent, towering spherical
To apices ever shifting.

3. The Singer Building or Singer Tower was a forty-one-story office building at Liberty Street and Broadway completed in 1908 as the headquarters of the Singer Manufacturing Company—maker of the sewing machines used in the sweatshops of the Ghetto. The building was demolished in 1968. The "idol's eye" is presumably the large semicircular structure that was visible on each side of the cupola at the top of the building's very high tower (in 1908 the highest in the world), which rose precipitously over a squared-off lower structure.

Broadway

Light![1]
Innumerable ions of light,
Kindling, irradiating,
All to their foci tending . . .

Light that jingles like anklet chains
On bevies of little lithe twinkling feet,
Or clingles in myriad vibrations[2]
Like trillions of porcelain
Vases shattering . . .

Light over the laminae of roofs,
Diffusing in shimmering nebulae
About the night's boundaries,
Or billowing in pearly foam
Submerging the low-lying stars . . .

Light for the feast prolonged—
Captive light in the goblets quivering . . .
Sparks evanescent

1. Broadway was the city's most illuminated avenue; it had been nicknamed "the Great White Way" as early as 1902 for the extravagant profusion of its lights. By 1910, there were over forty theaters with brightly illuminated marquees within a thirteen-block radius of Times Square.

2. "Clingle": a nonce word for "clink," also used later in the volume in "'The Everlasting Return.'"

Struck of meeting looks—
Fringed eyelids leashing
Sheathed and leaping lights . . .
Infinite bubbles of light
Bursting, reforming . . .
Silvery filings of light
Incessantly falling . . .
Scintillant, sided dust of light
Out of the white flares of Broadway—
Like a great spurious diamond
In the night's corsage faceted . . .

Broadway,
In ambuscades of light,
Drawing the charmed multitudes
With the slow suction of her breath—
Dangling her naked soul
Behind the blinding gold of eunuch lights
That wind about her like a bodyguard.

Or like a huge serpent, iridescent-scaled,
Trailing her coruscating length
Over the night prostrate—
Triumphant poised,
Her hydra heads above the avenues,
Values appraising
And her avid eyes
Glistening with eternal watchfulness . . .

Broadway—
Out of her towers rampant,
Like an unsubtle courtezan
Reserving nought for some adventurous night.

Flotsam

Crass rays streaming from the vestibules;
Cafes glittering like jeweled teeth;
High-flung signs
Blinking yellow phosphorescent eyes;
Girls in black
Circling monotonously
About the orange lights . . .

Nothing to guess at . . .
Save the darkness above
Crouching like a great cat.

In the dim-lit square,
Where disheveled trees
Tussle[1] with the wind—the wind like a scythe
Mowing their last leaves—
Arcs shimmering through a greenish haze—
Pale oval arcs
Like ailing virgins,
Each out of a halo circumscribed,
Pallidly staring . . .

Figures drift upon the benches

1. The published text gives "tustle."

With no more rustle than a dropped leaf settling—
Slovenly figures like untied parcels,
And papers wrapped about their knees
Huddled one to the other,
Cringing to the wind—
The sided wind,
Leaving no breach untried . . .

So many and all so still . . .
The fountain slobbering its stone basin
Is louder than They—
Flotsam of the five oceans
Here on this raft of the world.

This old man's head
Has found a woman's shoulder.
The wind juggles with her shawl
That flaps about them like a sail,
And splashes her red faded hair
Over the salt stubble of his chin.
A light foam is on his lips,
As though dreams surged in him
Breaking and ebbing away . . .
And the bare boughs shuffle above him
And the twigs rattle like dice . . .

She—diffused like a broken beetle—
Sprawls without grace,
Her face gray as asphalt,
Her jaws sagging as on loosened hinges . . .
Shadows ply about her mouth—

Nimble shadows out of the jigging tree,
That dances above her its dance of dry bones.[2]

II
A uniformed front,
Paunched;
A glance like a blow,
The swing of an arm,
Verved, vigorous;
Boot-heels clanking
In metallic rhythm;
The blows of a baton,
Quick, staccato . . .

—There is a rustling along the benches
As of dried leaves raked over . . .
And the old man lifts a shaking palsied hand,
Tucking the displaced paper about his knees.

Colder . . .
And a frost under foot,
Acid, corroding,
Eating through worn bootsoles.

Drab forms blur into greenish vapor.
Through boughs like cross-bones,
Pale arcs flare and shiver

2. "Dry bones": together with the wind in the branches, an allusion, laden with
irony, to Ezekiel 37:1–9. The passage begins, "The hand of the Lord was upon me . .
. and set me down in the midst of the valley which was full of bones," and concludes,
"Then said he unto me, Prophesy unto the wind, prophesy, son of man, and say
to the wind, Thus saith the Lord God; Come from the four winds, O breath, and
breathe upon these slain, that they may live."

Like lilies in a wind.

High over Broadway
A far-flung sign
Glitters in indigo darkness
And spurts again rhythmically,
Spraying great drops
Red as a hemorrhage.[3]

3. Readers today might take this stanza (echoing the image in lines 3–4) to be a description of a neon sign, and it almost is; the reference is to the earlier Moore lamp (named for its inventor, Daniel Moore), which also creates a glow when an electric current passes through gas-filled tubes. The sign is a measure of advancing modernity; the commercial use of Moore lamps was still new in 1918. (Neon began to replace them in 1923.)

Spring

A spring wind on the Bowery,
Blowing the fluff of night shelters
Off bedraggled garments,
And agitating the gutters, that eject little spirals of vapor
Like lewd growths.

Bare-legged children stamp in the puddles, splashing each other,
One—with a choir-boy's face
Twits me as I pass . . .
The word, like a muddied drop,
Seems to roll over and not out of
The bowed lips,
Yet dewy red
And sweetly immature.

People sniff the air with an upward look—
Even the mite of a girl
Who never plays . . .
Her mother smiles at her
With eyes like vacant lots
Rimming vistas of mean streets
And endless washing days . . .
Yet with sun on the lines
And a drying breeze.

The old candy woman
Shivers in the young wind.
Her eyes—littered with memories
Like ancient garrets,
Or dusty unaired rooms where someone died—
Ask nothing of the spring.

But a pale pink dream
Trembles about this young girl's body,
Draping it like a glowing aura.

She gloats in a mirror
Over her gaudy hat,
With its flower God never thought of . . .

And the dream, unrestrained,
Floats about the loins of a soldier,
Where it quivers a moment,
Warming to a crimson
Like the scarf of a toreador . . .[1]

But the delicate gossamer breaks at his contact
And recoils to her in strands of shattered rose.

1. Probably an allusion to the refrain of the Toreador's song in Georges Bizet's
opera *Carmen* (1875):

> And dream away, yes, dream in combat,
> That a black eye is watching you
> And that love awaits you,
> Toreador, love awaits you!

Bowery Afternoon

Drab discoloration
Of faces, façades, pawn-shops,
Second-hand clothing,
Smoky and fly-blown glass of lunch-rooms,
Odors of rancid life . . .

Deadly uniformity
Of eyes and windows
Alike devoid of light . . .
Holes wherein life scratches—
Mangy life
Nosing to the gutter's end . . .

Show-rooms and mimic pillars
Flaunting out of their gaudy vestibules
Bosoms and posturing thighs . . .

Over all the Elevated
Droning like a bloated fly.[1]

1. The elevated train line (the "El") running along the Bowery to Astor Place
was opened in 1878 with disastrous consequences. The noise and dirt of the trains
prompted a steep fall in property values and the growth of saloons and cheap lodg-
ing houses, "pawn-shops, [and] / second-hand clothing," precipitating the street's
long-lasting reputation as a skid row. In 1913 Theodore Roosevelt wrote that the
"seething life" of the Bowery was "haunted by demons as evil as any that stalk
through the pages of the *Inferno*" (Nevlus 2017).

Undulant rustlings,
Of oncoming silk,
Rhythmic, incessant,
Like the motion of leaves . . .
Fragments of color
In glowing surprises . . .
Pink innuendoes
Hooded in gray
Like buds in a cobweb
Pearled at dawn . . .
Glimpses of green
And blurs of gold
And delicate mauves
That snatch at youth . . .
And bodies all rosily
Fleshed for the airing,
In warm velvety surges
Passing imperious, slow . . .

Women drift into the limousines
That shut like silken caskets
On gems half weary of their glittering . . .
Lamps open like pale moon flowers . . .
Arcs are radiant opals
Strewn along the dusk . . .

No common lights invade.
And spires rise like litanies—
Magnificats of stone
Over the white silence of the arcs,
Burning in perpetual adoration.

Out of the lamp-bestarred and clouded dusk—
Snaring, eluding,[1] concealing,
Magically conjuring—
Turning to fairy-coaches
Beetle-backed limousines
Scampering under the great Arch—[2]
Making a decoy of blue overalls
And mystery of a scarlet shawl—
Indolently—
Knowing no impediment of its sure advance—
Descends the fog.

1. The published text gives "illuding." "Eluding" fits the context of mystery better than "alluding," although either is possible.
2. The arch at the Fifth Avenue entry to Washington Square Park, designed by Stanford White in 1891 and open to traffic until 1952.

A late snow beats
With cold white fists upon the tenements—
Hurriedly drawing blinds and shutters,
Like tall old slatterns
Pulling aprons about their heads.

Lights slanting out of Mott Street
Gibber out,
Or dribble through bar-room slits,
Anonymous shapes
Conniving behind shuttered panes
Caper and disappear . . .
Where the Bowery
Is throbbing like a fistula
Back of her ice-scabbed fronts.

Livid faces
Glimmer in furtive doorways,
Or spill out of the black pockets of alleys,
Smears of faces like muddied beads,
Making a ghastly rosary
The night mumbles over
And the snow with its devilish and silken whisper . . .
Patrolling arcs

Blowing shrill blasts over the Bread Line[1]
Stalk them as they pass,
Silent as though accouched of the darkness,
And the wind noses among them,
    Like a skunk
That roots about the heart . . .

Colder:
And the Elevated slams upon the silence
Like a ponderous door.
Then all is still again,
Save for the wind fumbling over
The emptily swaying faces—
The wind rummaging
Like an old Jew . . .

Faces in glimmering rows . . .
(No sign of the abject life—
Not even a blasphemy . . .)
But the spindle legs keep time
To a limping rhythm,
And the shadows twitch upon the snow
    Convulsively—
As though death played
With some ungainly dolls.

1. "Bread Line": the Bowery Mission (founded in 1879 and still in operation) maintained a much-frequented soup kitchen that remained open into the small hours of the night.

FIGURE 6. Bowery bread line, 1910. Library of Congress.

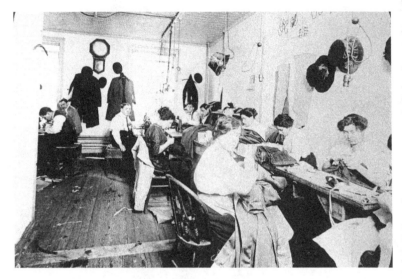

FIGURE 7. A small sweatshop, 1910. Photograph by Louis Hine. Courtesy of the Kheel Center for Labor-Management Documentation and Archives, Cornell University.

Labor

Debris

I love those spirits
That men stand off and point at,
Or shudder and hood up their souls—
Those ruined ones,
Where Liberty has lodged an hour
And passed like flame,
Bursting asunder the too small house.

I would be a torch unto your hand,
A lamp upon your forehead, Labor,
In the wild darkness before the Dawn
That I shall never see . . .

We shall advance together, my Beloved,
Awaiting the mighty ushering . . .
Together we shall make the last grand charge
And ride with gorgeous Death
With all her spangles on
And cymbals clashing . . .
And you shall rush on exultant as I fall—
Scattering a brief fire about your feet . . .

Let it be so . . .
Better—while life is quick
And every pain immense and joy supreme,
And all I have and am
Flames upward to the dream . . .
Than like a taper forgotten in the dawn,
Burning out the wick.

The Song of Iron[1]

I

Not yet hast Thou sounded
Thy clangorous music,
Whose strings are under the mountains . . .[2]
Not yet hast Thou spoken
The blooded, implacable Word . . .

But I hear in the Iron singing—
In the triumphant roaring of the steam and pistons pounding—
Thy barbaric exhortation . . .
And the blood leaps in my arteries, unreproved,
Answering Thy call . . .
All my spirit is inundated with the tumultuous passion of Thy Voice,
And sings exultant with the Iron,
For now I know I too am of Thy Chosen . . .

1. The use of iron as the symbol of industrial labor probably stems from the prominence of iron- and steelworkers' unions in the history of the labor movement. The history was one of recurrent violence and defeat. Its turning point was the infamous Homestead Strike of 1892, an action in Pittsburgh against Carnegie Steel that culminated in a bloody firefight and broke the back of the Amalgamated Association of Iron and Steel Workers, formerly known as the Sons of Vulcan.

2. The strings under the mountain are the veins of iron ore. The image may link the "song" of iron to a symbolic source as well as to the material clangor of metalwork. Legend has it that Pythagoras discovered the basis of musical tuning by listening to the strokes of four blacksmith's hammers. The whole-number ratios involved are actually produced by vibrating strings.

Oh fashioned in fire—
Needing flame for Thy ultimate word—[3]
Behold me, a cupola[4]
Poured to Thy use!

Heed not my tremulous body
That faints in the grip of Thy gauntlet.
Break it . . . and cast it aside . . .
But make of my spirit
That dares and endures
Thy crucible . . .
Pour through my soul
Thy molten, world-whelming song.

   . . . Here at Thy uttermost gate
Like a new Mary, I wait . . .

II
Charge the blast furnace, workman . . .
Open the valves—
Drive the fires high . . .
(Night is above the gates).

How golden-hot the ore is
From the cupola spurting,
Tossing the flaming petals
Over the silt and furnace ash—

3. The fires of the iron foundries transmit the divine Word on the model of their biblical forebears: the burning bush through which God speaks to Moses (Exodus 3:1–4), the coal placed on the prophet Isaiah's tongue (Isaiah 6:6–8), and the Pentecostal tongues of fire that descend on Christ's apostles (Acts 2:1–4; see also note 9, below).

4. "Cupola": A cylindrical blast furnace capable of melting iron.

Blown leaves, devastating,
Falling about the world . . .

Out of the furnace mouth—
Out of the giant mouth—
The raging, turgid, mouth—
Fall fiery blossoms
Gold with the gold of buttercups
In a field at sunset,
Or huskier gold of dandelions,
Warmed in sun-leavings,
Or changing to the paler hue
At the creamy hearts of primroses.

Charge the converter,[5] workman—
Tired from the long night?
But the earth shall suck up darkness—
The earth that holds so much . . .
And out of these molten flowers,
Shall shape the heavy fruit . . .

Then open the valves—
Drive the fires high,
Your blossoms nurturing.
(Day is at the gates
And a young wind . . .)

Put by your rod,[6] comrade,
And look with me, shading your eyes . . .
Do you not see—
Through the lucent haze

5. "Converter": a Bessemer furnace, used to convert molten iron to steel.
6. "Rod": an ingot of crude iron ("pig iron") to be fed into the converter.

Out of the converter rising—
In the spirals of fire
Smiting and blinding,
A shadowy shape
White as a flame of sacrifice,
Like a lily swaying?

III
The ore leaping in the crucibles,
The ore communicant,
Sending faint thrills along the leads . . .
Fire is running along the roots of the mountains . . .
I feel the long recoil of earth
As under a mighty quickening . . .
(Dawn is aglow in the light of the Iron . . .)
All palpitant, I wait . . .

IV
Hear[7] ye, Dictators—late Lords of the Iron,
Shut in your council rooms, palsied, depowered—
The blooded, implacable Word?
Not whispered in cloture,[8] one to the other,
(Brother in fear of the fear of his brother . . .)
But chanted and thundered
On the brazen, articulate tongues of the Iron

7. The published text gives "Here," clearly a misprint.
8. The context suggests that "in cloture" here means something like "in camera," that is, out of public hearing; the poem elevates the Word from an utterance to a roar. The closing down of parliamentary debate would thus serve as a metaphor for the attempt by the Lords of Iron to silence the unwelcome voices of their workers. Ridge may be thinking of the cloture rule adopted by Britain's House of Commons in 1882 in order to overcome the obstructionist tactics of the Irish Parliamentary Party under Charles Stewart Parnell.

Babbling in flame . . .[9]
Sung to the rhythm of prisons dismantled,
Manacles riven and ramparts defaced . . .
(Hearts death-anointed yet hearing life calling . . .)
Ankle chains bursting and gallows unbraced . . .

Sung to the rhythm of arsenals burning . . .
Clangor of iron smashing on iron,
Turmoil of metal and dissonant baying
Of mail-sided monsters shattered asunder . . .

Hulks of black turbines all mangled and roaring,
Battering egress through ramparted walls . . .
Mouthing of engines, made rabid with power,
Into the holocaust snorting and plunging . . .

Mighty converters torn from their axis,
Flung to the furnaces, vomiting fire,
Jumbled in white-heaten masses disshapen . . .
Writhing in flame-tortured levers of iron . . .
Gnashing of steel serpents twisting and dying . . .
Screeching of steam-glutted cauldrons rending . . .
Shock of leviathans prone on each other . . .
Scaled flanks touching, ore entering ore . . .
Steel haunches closing and grappling and swaying
In the waltz of the mating locked mammoths of iron,
Tasting the turbulent fury of living,
Mad with a moment's exuberant living!

9. "Babbling in flame": an allusion to Pentecost, Acts 2:3–4: "And there appeared unto them [the apostles] cloven tongues like as of fire, and it sat upon each of them. And they were all filled with the Holy Ghost, and began to speak with other tongues, as the Spirit gave them utterance."

Crash of devastating hammers despoiling...
Hands inexorable, marring
What hands had so cunningly molded . . .

Structures of steel welded, subtily tempered,
Marvelous wrought of the wizards of ore,
Torn into octaves discordantly clashing,
Chords never final but onward progressing
In monstrous fusion of sound ever smiting on sound
        in mad vortices whirling . . .

Till the ear, tortured, shrieks for cessation
Of the raving inharmonies hatefully mingling . . .
The fierce obbligato the steel pipes are screaming . . .
The blare of the rude molten music of Iron . . .

Frank Little at Calvary[1]

I
He walked under the shadow of the Hill
Where men are fed into the fires
And walled apart . . .
Unarmed and alone,
He summoned his mates from the pit's mouth
Where tools rested on the floors
And great cranes swung
Unemptied, on the iron girders.
And they, who were the Lords of the Hill,
Were seized with a great fear,
When they heard out of the silence of wheels
The answer ringing
In endless reverberations
Under the mountain . . .

1. Frank Little: American labor leader, known as "the hobo agitator," murdered in Butte, Montana, in August 1917. The murderers remain unknown, though most historians think they were hired by the copper mining company, Anaconda, which was responsible for a disaster in June 1917 that killed 168 miners and brought Little to Butte in July. The second stanza gives an accurate account of Little's abduction. See Carroll 2016.

"Calvary," because the mine in Butte lay under what was called "the richest hill on earth"; the Hill thus merges with the site outside the gates of Jerusalem, also called Golgotha, the "place of the skull," traditionally represented as a hill, where Jesus was crucified.

So they covered up their faces
And crept upon him as he slept . . .
Out of eye-holes in black cloth
They looked upon him who had flung
Between them and their ancient prey
The frail barricade of his life . . .
And when night—that has connived at so much—
Was heavy with the unborn day,
They haled him[2] from his bed . . .

Who might know of that wild ride?
Only the bleak Hill—
The red Hill, vigilant,
Like a blood-shot eye
In the black mask of night—
Dared watch them as they raced
By each blind-folded street
Godiva might have ridden down . . .
But when they stopped beside the Place,
I know he turned his face
Wistfully to the accessory night . . .

And when he saw—against the sky,
Sagged like a silken net
Under its load of stars—
The black bridge poised
Like a gigantic spider motionless . . .
I know there was a silence in his heart,
As of a frozen sea,
Where some half lifted arm, mid-way

2. "Haled him": forcibly dragged him; a rare usage.

Wavers, and drops heavily . . .[3]

I know he waved to life,
And that life signaled back, transcending space,
To each high-powered sense,
So that he missed no gesture of the wind
Drawing the shut leaves close . . .
So that he saw the light on comrades' faces
Of camp fires out of sight . . .
And the savor of meat and bread
Blew in his nostrils . . . and the breath
Of unrailed spaces
Where shut wild clover smelled as sweet
As a virgin in her bed.

I know he looked once at America,
Quiescent, with her great flanks on the globe,
And once at the skies whirling above him . . .
Then all that he had spoken against
And struck against and thrust against
Over the frail barricade of his life
Rushed between him and the stars . . .

II
Life thunders on . . .
Over the black bridge
The line of lighted cars
Creeps like a monstrous serpent
Spooring gold . . .

3. Little was hanged from a railroad trestle. He was probably already dead by
then, but Ridge could not have known that.

Watchman, what of the track?[4]

Night . . . silence . . . stars . . .
All's Well!

III
Light . . .
(Breaking mists . . .
Hills gliding like hands out of a slipping hold . . .)
Light over the pit mouths,
Streaming in tenuous rays down the black gullets of the Hill . . .
(The copper, insensate, sleeping in the buried lode.)
Light . . .
Forcing the clogged windows of arsenals . . .
Probing with long sentient fingers in the copper chips . . .
Gleaming metallic and cold
In numberless slivers of steel . . .
Light over the trestles and the iron clips
Of the black bridge—poised like a gigantic spider motionless—
Sweet inquisition of light, like a child's wonder . . .
Intrusive, innocently staring light
That nothing appalls . . .

Light in the slow fumbling summer leaves,

4. An echo of the line "Watchman, What of the Night?" from Isaiah 21:11–12: "The burden of Dumah. He calleth to me out of Seir, Watchman, what of the night? Watchman, what of the night? The watchman said, The morning cometh, and also the night: if ye will enquire, enquire ye: return, come." The reference may extend to the hymn "Watchman, What of the Night?" (1871) by Sir Arthur Sullivan. Sullivan's musical setting alternates reassuring answers from the chorus with troubled questions about mortality from the soloists: "But, watchman, what of the night, / When the arrow of death is sped, / And the grave, which no glimm'ring star can light, / Shall be my sleeping bed?" (Gilbert and Sullivan Archive, 1993, 2006, www. gsarchive.net/sullivan/part_songs/watchman/watchman.html).

Cooing and calling
All winged and avid things
Waking the early flies, keen to the scent . . .
Green-jeweled iridescent flies
Unerringly steering—
Swarming over the blackened lips,
The young day sprays with indiscriminate gold . . .

Watchman, what of the Hill?

Wheels turn;
The laden cars
Go rumbling to the mill,
And Labor walks beside the mules . . .
All's Well with the Hill!

Spires of Grace Church,[1]
For you the workers of the world
Travailed with the mountains . . .
Aborting their own dreams
Till the dream of you arose—
Beautiful, swaddled in stone—
Scorning their hands.

1. Episcopal church on Broadway in Lower Manhattan. Constructed in 1846, the church features numerous spires, including a very high primary spire; compare the Church of St. Theresa in "The Ghetto."

The Legion of Iron

They pass through the great iron gates—-
Men with eyes gravely discerning,
Skilled to appraise the tonnage of cranes
Or split an inch into thousandths—
Men tempered by fire as the ore is
And planned to resistance
Like steel that has cooled in the trough;
Silent of purpose, inflexible, set to fulfilment—
To conquer, withstand, overthrow . . .
Men mannered to large undertakings,
Knowing force as a brother
And power as something to play with,
Seeing blood as a slip of the iron,
To be wiped from the tools
Lest they rust.

But what if they stood aside,
Who hold the earth so careless in the crook of their arms?

What of the flamboyant cities
And the lights guttering out like candles in a wind . . .
And the armies halted . . .
And the train mid-way on the mountain
And idle men chaffing across the trenches . . .
And the cursing and lamentation

And the clamor for grain shut in the mills of the world?
What if they stayed apart,
Inscrutably smiling,
Leaving the ground encumbered with dead wire
And the sea to row-boats
And the lands marooned—
Till Time should like a paralytic sit,
A mildewed hulk above the nations squatting?

Fuel

What of the silence of the keys
And silvery hands? The iron sings . . .
Though bows lie broken on the strings,
The fly-wheels turn eternally . . .

Bring fuel—drive the fires high . . .
Throw all this artist-lumber in
And foolish dreams of making things . . .
(Ten million men are called to die.)

As for the common men apart,
Who sweat to keep their common breath,
And have no hour for books or art—
What dreams have these to hide from death!

Not your martyrs anointed of heaven—
    The ages are red where they trod—
But the Hunted—the world's bitter leaven—
    Who smote at your imbecile God—

A being to pander and fawn to,
    To propitiate, flatter and dread
As a thing that your souls are in pawn to,
    A Dealer who traffics the dead;

A Trader with greed never sated,
    Who barters the souls in his snares,
That were trapped in the lusts he created,
    For incense and masses and prayers—

They are crushed in the coils of your halters;
    'Twere well—by the creeds ye have nursed—
That ye send up a cry from your altars,
    A mass for the Martyrs Accursed;

A passionate prayer from reprieval
    For the Brotherhood not understood—
For the Heroes who died for the evil,
    Believing the evil was good.

To the Breakers, the Bold, the Despoilers,
     Who dreamed of a world over-thrown . . .
They who died for the millions of toilers—
     Few—fronting the nations alone!

—To the Outlawed of men and the Branded,
     Whether hated or hating they fell—
I pledge the devoted, red-handed,
     Unfaltering Heroes of Hell!

Accidentals

"The Everlasting Return"[1]

It is dark . . . so dark, I remember the sun on Chios . . .[2]
It is still . . . so still, I hear the beat of our paddles on the Aegean . . .

Ten times we had watched the moon
Rise like a thin white virgin out of the waters
And round into a full maternity . . .
For thrice ten moons we had touched no flesh
Save the man flesh on either hand
That was black and bitter and salt and scaled by the sea.

The Athenian boy sat on my left . . .
His hair was yellow as corn steeped in wine . . .
And on my right was Phildar the Carthaginian,
Grinning Phildar
With his mouth pulled taut as by reins from his black gapped teeth.[3]

1. The use of this quoted phrase to refer to Nietzsche's concept of the eternal return suggests that Ridge had read Georges Chatterton-Hill's *The Philosophy of Nietzsche*, published in 1914. Chatterton-Hill writes (incorrectly) that "the vision of Beauty incarnated in the Over-Man is such that it makes us ardently desire the everlasting return of all things" (260). Ridge's allusion is ironic; the poem depicts the everlasting return of war by fusing the deaths in battle of three ancient galley slaves and three submariners in World War I.

2. Chios is said to be the birthplace of Homer.

3. The seating arrangement identifies the ship as a trireme, propelled by banks of three oars on either side. That the slaves are Greek and Carthaginian identifies the trireme as Roman and the date as some time after the Roman destruction of Carthage in 146 BCE.

Many a whip had coiled about him
And his shoulders were rutted deep as wet ground under chariot wheels,
And his skin was red and tough as a bull's hide cured in the sun.
He did not sing like the other slaves,
But when a big wind came up he screamed with it.
And always he looked out to sea,
Save when he tore at his fish ends
Or spat across me at the Greek boy, whose mouth was red and apart
    like an opened fruit.

We had rowed from dawn and the green galley hard at our stern.
She was green and squat and skulked close to the sea.
All day the tish of their paddles had tickled our ears,[4]
And when night came on
And little naked stars dabbled in the water
And half the crouching moon
Slid over the silver belly of the sea thick-scaled with light,
We heard them singing at their oars . . .
We who had no breath for song.

There was no sound in our boat
Save the clingle of wrist chains
And the sobbing of the young Greek.
I cursed him that his hair blew in my mouth, tasting salt of the sea . . .
I cursed him that his oar kept ill time . . .
When he looked at me I cursed him again,
That his eyes were soft as a woman's.

How long . . . since their last shell gouged our batteries?
How long . . . since we rose at aim with a sleuth moon astern?
(It was the damned green moon that nosed us out . . .

4. "Tish": like "clingle" below, an onomatopoetic nonce word.

The moon that flushed our periscope till it shone like a silver flame . . .)[5]

They loosed each man's right hand
As the galley spent on our decks . . .
And amazed and bloodied we reared half up
And fought askew with the left hand shackled . . .
But a zigzag fire leapt in our sockets
And knotted our thews like string . . .
Our thews grown stiff as a crooked spine that would not straighten . . .

How long . . . since our gauges fell
And the sea shoved us under?
It is dark . . . so dark . . .
Darkness presses hairy-hot
Where three make crowded company . . .
And the rank steel smells . . .
It is still . . . so still . . .
I seem to hear the wind
On the dimpled face of the water fathoms above . . .

It was still . . . so still . . . we three that were left alive
Stared in each other's faces . . .
But three make bitter company at one man's bread . . .
And our hate grew sharp and bright as the moon's edge in the water.
One grinned with his mouth awry from the long gapped teeth . . .
And one shivered and whined like a gull as the waves pawed us over . . .
But one struck with his hate in his hand . . .

After that I remember

5. Although the German U-boat remains iconic for submarine warfare in World War I, the Western allies, especially the British, also deployed submarines—at great cost in lives and materiel. By the end of the war the British had lost more than a third of their submarine fleet.

Only the dead men's oars that flapped in the sea . . .
The dead men's oars that rattled and clicked like idiots' tongues.

It is still . . . so still, with the jargon of engines quiet.
We three awaiting the crunch of the sea
Reach our hands in the dark and touch each other's faces . . .
We three sheathing hate in our hearts . . .
But when hate shall have made its circuit,
Our bones will be loving company
Here in the sea's den . . .
And one whimpers and cries on his God
And one sits sullenly
But both draw away from me . . .
For I am the pyre their memories burn on . . .
Like black flames leaping
Our fiery gestures light the walled-in darkness of the sea . . .
The sea that kneels above us . . .
And makes no sign.

Palestine

Old plant of Asia—[1]
Mutilated vine
Holding earth's leaping sap
In every stem and shoot
That lopped off, sprouts again—
Why should you seek a plateau walled about,
Whose garden is the world?

1. Prior to World War I, Palestine was an outpost of the Ottoman Empire with a small Jewish population. When the war ended, control passed to the British, who in 1917 had issued a public pledge—the "Balfour Declaration," named for the British Foreign Secretary who issued it—to make the territory "a national home for the Jewish people." The poem's two final lines seem to oppose the proposed homeland ("a plateau walled about") to the Jewish diaspora ("whose garden is the world").

That day, in the slipping of torsos and straining flanks
    on the bloodied ooze of fields plowed by the iron,
And the smoke bluish near earth and bronze in the sunshine
    floating like cotton-down,
And the harsh and terrible screaming,
And that strange vibration at the roots of us . . .
Desire, fierce, like a song . . .
And we heard
(Do you remember?)
All the Red Cross bands on Fifth Avenue[1]
And bugles in little home towns
And children's harmonicas bleating

America!

And after . . .
(Do you remember?)
The drollery of the wind on our faces,
And horizons reeling,
And the terror of the plain
Heaving like a gaunt pelvis to the sun . . .
Under us—threshing and twanging
Torn-up roots of the Song . . .

1. On October 4, 1917, 15,000 uniformed nurses from the American Red Cross paraded in serried ranks down New York's Fifth Avenue (a frequent site for patriotic parades at the time) in support of the war effort.

To the Others

I see you, refulgent ones,
Burning so steadily
Like big white arc lights . . .
There are so many of you.
I like to watch you weaving—
Altogether and with precision
Each his ray—
Your tracery of light,
Making a shining way about America.

I note your infinite reactions—
In glassware
And sequin
And puddles
And bits of jet—
And here and there a diamond . . .

But you do not yet see me,
Who am a torch blown along the wind,
Flickering to a spark
But never out.

Babel

Oh, God did cunningly, there at Babel—
Not mere tongues dividing, but soul from soul,
So that never again should men be able
To fashion one infinite, towering whole.[1]

1. The biblical story of "the city and the tower" of Babel, Genesis 11:1–9, is best known for its explanation of the multiplicity of languages. Ridge dwells instead on God's determination to keep humanity disunited. The people built the city and tower "lest we be scattered abroad upon the face of the whole earth"—which is exactly what happens: "So the LORD scattered them abroad from thence upon the face of all the earth: and they left off to build the city."

The Fiddler

In a little Hungarian cafe
Men and women are drinking
Yellow wine in tall goblets.

Through the milky haze of the smoke,
The fiddler, under-sized, blond,
Leans to his violin
As to the breast of a woman.
Red hair kindles to fire
On the black of his coat-sleeve,
Where his white thin hand
Trembles and dives,
Like a sliver of moonlight,
When wind has broken the water.

Dawn Wind[1]

Wind, just arisen—
(Off what cool mattress of marsh-moss
In tented boughs leaf-drawn before the stars,
Or niche of cliff under the eagles?)
You of living things,
So gay and tender and full of play—
Why do you blow on my thoughts—like cut flowers
Gathered and laid to dry on this paper, rolled out of dead wood?

 I see you
 Shaking that flower at me with soft invitation
And frisking away,
Deliciously rumpling the grass . . .

So you fluttered the curtains about my cradle,
Prattling of fields
Before I had had my milk . . .
Did I stir on my pillow, making to follow you, Fleet One?
I—swaddled, unwinged, like a bird in the egg.

Let be
My dreams that crackle under your breath . . .

1. The first of three successive lyrics conceived partly as a revocation of Percy Bysshe Shelley's "Ode to the West Wind" (1819).

You have the dust of the world to blow on . . .
Do not tag me and dance away, looking back . . .
I am too old to play with you,
Eternal Child.

I love you, malcontent
Male wind—
Shaking the pollen from a flower
Or hurling the sea backward from the grinning sand.[1]

Blow on and over my dreams . . .
Scatter my sick dreams . . .
Throw your lusty arms about me . . .
Envelop all my hot body . . .
Carry me to pine forests—
Great, rough-bearded forests . . .
Bring me to stark plains and steppes . . .
I would have the North to-night—
The cold, enduring North.

And if we should meet the Snow,
Whirling in spirals,
And he should blind my eyes . . .
Ally, you will defend me—
You will hold me close,
Blowing on my eyelids.

1. Compare Shelley's "Ode": "Thou / For whose path the Atlantic's level powers / Cleave themselves into chasms" (lines 36–38).

The Destroyer

I am of the wind . . .
A wisp of the battering wind . . .

I trail my fingers along the Alps
And an avalanche falls in my wake . . .[1]
I feel in my quivering length
When it buries the hamlet beneath . . .

I hurriedly sweep aside
The cities that clutter our path . . .
As we whirl about the circle of the globe . . .
As we tear at the pillars of the world . . .
Open to the wind,
The Destroyer![2]
The wind that is battering at your gates.

1. Compare Shelley's prefatory note: "That tempestuous wind . . . was collecting
the vapours which pour down the autumnal rains . . . attended by that magnificent
thunder and lightning peculiar to the cisalpine regions."
2. This return to the title phrase echoes Shelley with a pointed omission: "Wild
spirit which art moving everywhere, / Destroyer and preserver; hear, oh hear!" (lines
13–14). Ridge's battering wind presumably still blows from the North, obliterating
any trace of the gentle breeze rejected in "Dawn Wind." "The Destroyer" thus
reverses the famous conclusion of Shelley's Ode: "O, wind, / If winter comes, can
spring be far behind?" (lines 69–70).

Lullaby[1]

Rock-a-by baby, woolly and brown . . .
(There's a shout at the door an' a big red light . . .)
Lil' coon baby, mammy is down . . .
Han's that hold yuh are steady an' white . . .

Look piccaninny—such a gran' blaze
Lickin' up the roof an' the sticks of home—
Ever see the like in all yo' days!
—Cain't yuh sleep, mah bit-of-honey-comb?

Rock-a-by baby, up to the sky!
Look at the cherries driftin' by—
Bright red cherries spilled on the groun'—
Piping-hot cherries at nuthin' a poun'!

---

1. As Ridge explains in the parenthetical note she appended to it, this dialect poem was meant to condemn an atrocity, the murder by fire of a Black infant during a racist "riot" by whites. The violence, more massacre than riot, broke out amid labor unrest in East St. Louis, Illinois, in July 1917. White mobs rampaged through the streets beating and shooting Black residents indiscriminately. The death toll remains unknown; the NAACP estimated it at the time as between one hundred and two hundred. Black neighborhoods were torched as well, leaving six thousand people homeless.

Ridge's adoption of a Black voice speaking in dialect, however well intentioned, remains hard to justify. Even the use of dialect by Black poets sparked objection by critics in the early twentieth century who argued that no use of dialect could escape plantation stereotypes (Gates 1987, 165–95).

Hush, mah lil' black-bug—doan yuh weep.
Daddy's run away an' mammy's in a heap
By her own fron' door in the blazin' heat
Outah the shacks like warts on the street . . .

An' the singin' flame an' the gleeful crowd
Circlin' aroun' . . . won't mammy be proud!
With a stone at her hade an' a stone on her heart,
An' her mouth like a red plum, broken apart . . .

See where the blue an' khaki prance,
Adding brave colors to the dance
About the big bonfire white folks make—
Such gran' doin's fo' a lil' coon's sake!

Hear all the eagah feet runnin' in town—
See all the willin' han's reach outah night—
Han's that are wonderful, steady an' white!
To toss up a lil' babe, blinkin' an' brown . . .

Rock-a-by baby—higher an' higher!
Mammy is sleepin' an' daddy's run lame . . .
(Soun' may yuh sleep in yo' cradle o' fire!)
Rock-a-by baby, hushed in the flame . . .

(An incident of the East St. Louis Race Riots, when some white women
flung a living colored baby into the heart of a blazing fire.)

The Foundling

Snow wraiths circle us
Like washers of the dead,
Flapping their white wet cloths
Impatiently
About the grizzled head,
Where the coarse hair mats like grass,
And the efficient wind
With cold professional baste
Probes like a lancet
Through the cotton shirt . . .

About us are white cliffs and space.
No façades show,
Nor roof nor any spire . . .
All sheathed in snow . . .
The parasitic snow
That clings about them like a blight.

Only detached lights
Float hazily like greenish moons,
And endlessly
Down the whore-street,
Accouched and comforted and sleeping warm,
The blizzard waltzes with the night.

The Woman with Jewels

The woman with jewels sits in the cafe,
Spraying light like a fountain.
Diamonds glitter on her bulbous fingers
And on her arms, great as thighs,
Diamonds gush from her ear-lobes over the goitrous throat.
She is obesely beautiful.
Her eyes are full of bleared lights,
Like little pools of tar, spilled by a sailor in mad haste for shore . . .
And her mouth is scarlet and full—only a little crumpled—
    like a flower that has been pressed apart . . .[1]

Why does she come alone to this obscure basement—
She who should have a litter and hand-maidens to support her
    on either side?

She ascends the stairway, and the waiters turn to look at her,
    spilling the soup.
The black satin dress is a little lifted, showing the dropsical legs
    in their silken fleshings . . .
The mountainous breasts tremble . . .
There is an agitation in her gems,

1. The woman with jewels and scarlet mouth recalls the "great whore"—the
Whore of Babylon—of Revelation 17:4: "And the woman was arrayed in purple and
scarlet color, and decked with gold and precious stones and pearls, having a golden
cup in her hand full of abominations and filthiness of her fornication."

That quiver incessantly, emitting trillions of fiery rays . . .
She erupts explosive breaths . . .
Every step is an adventure
From this . . .
The serpent's tooth
Saved Cleopatra.[2]

2. Plutarch and other ancient historians report (but do not confirm) that Cleopatra killed herself after the death of Marc Antony by coaxing an asp (an Egyptian cobra) to bite her breast. Ridge's primary reference is probably to act 5, scene 2 of Shakespeare's *Antony and Cleopatra*; the phrase "serpent's tooth" is from *King Lear* (act 1, scene 4).

Submerged

I have known only my own shallows—
Safe, plumbed places,
Where I was wont to preen myself.

But for the abyss
I wanted a plank beneath
And horizons . . .

I was afraid of the silence
And the slipping toe-hold . . .

Oh, could I now dive
Into the unexplored deeps of me--
Delve and bring up and give
All that is submerged, encased, unfolded,
That is yet the best.

When Art goes bounding, lean,
Up hill-tops fired green
To pluck a rose for life.

Life like a broody hen
Cluck-clucks him back again.

But when Art, imbecile,
Sits old and chill
On sidings shaven clean,
And counts his clustering
Dead daisies on a string
With witless laughter . . .

Then like a new Jill
Toiling up a hill
Life scrambles after.

Brooklyn Bridge

Pythoness[1] body—arching
Over the night like an ecstasy—
I feel your coils tightening . . .
And the world's lessening breath.

1. "Pythoness": both a female serpent and the Pythia, the priestess at Delphi who conveyed the oracles of Apollo.

Men die . . .
Dreams only change their houses.
They cannot be lined up against a wall
And quietly buried under ground,
And no more heard of . . .
However deep the pit and heaped the clay—
Like seedlings of old time
Hooding a sacred rose under the ice cap of the world—
Dreams will to light.

The Fire

The old men of the world have made a fire
To warm their trembling hands.
They poke the young men in.
The young men burn like withes.[1]

If one run a little way,
The old men are wroth.[2]
They catch him and bind him and throw him again to the flames.
Green withes burn slow . . .
And the smoke of the young men's torment
Rises round and sheer as the trunk of a pillared oak,[3]
And the darkness thereof spreads over the sky . . .

Green withes burn slow . . .
And the old men of the world sit round the fire
And rub their hands . . .
But the smoke of the young men's torment
Ascends up for ever and ever.

1. According to ancient historians, the druids of Celtic Britain (high officials including priests) engaged in human sacrifice by methods that included burning the victim within an effigy woven of wicker (withes).

2. The published text gives "wrath."

3. The oak tree was sacred in Celtic religion; oak groves were reputedly used as sites for druidic sacrifice.

I remember
The crackle of the palm trees
Over the mooned white roofs of the town . . .
The shining town . . .
And the tender fumbling of the surf
On the sulphur-yellow beaches
As we sat . . . a little apart . . . in the close-pressing night.

The moon hung above us like a golden mango,
And the moist air clung to our faces,
Warm and fragrant as the open mouth of a child
And we watched the out-flung sea
Rolling to the purple edge of the world,
Yet ever back upon itself . . .
As we . . .

Inadequate night . . .
And mooned white memory
Of a tropic sea . . .
How softly it comes up
Like an ungathered lily.

The Edge

I thought to die that night in the solitude where they would never find
     me . . .
But there was time . . .
And I lay quietly on the drawn knees of the mountain,
     staring into the abyss . . .
I do not know how long . . .
I could not count the hours, they ran so fast
Like little bare-foot urchins—shaking my hands away . . .
But I remember
Somewhere water trickled like a thin severed vein . . .
And a wind came out of the grass,
Touching me gently, tentatively, like a paw.

As the night grew
The gray cloud that had covered the sky like sackcloth
Fell in ashen folds about the hills,
Like hooded virgins, pulling their cloaks about them . . .
There must have been a spent moon,
For the Tall One's veil held a shimmer of silver . . .

That too I remember . . .
And the tenderly rocking mountain
Silence
And beating stars . . .

Dawn
Lay like a waxen hand upon the world,
And folded hills
Broke into a sudden wonder of peaks, stemming clear and cold,
Till the Tall One bloomed like a lily,
Flecked with sun,
Fine as a golden pollen—
It seemed a wind might blow it from the snow.

I smelled the raw sweet essences of things,
And heard spiders in the leaves
And ticking of little feet,
As tiny creatures came out of their doors
To see God pouring light into his star . . .

. . . It seemed life held
No future and no past but this . . .

And I too got up stiffly from the earth,
And held my heart up like a cup . . .

The Garden

Bountiful Givers,
I look along the years
And see the flowers you threw . . .
Anemones
And sprigs of gray
Sparse heather of the rocks,
Or a wild violet
Or daisy of a daisied field . . .
But each your best.

I might have worn them on my breast
To wilt in the long day . . .
I might have stemmed them in a narrow vase
And watched each petal sallowing . . .
I might have held them so—mechanically—
Till the wind winnowed all the leaves
 And left upon my hands
 A little smear of dust.

Instead
I hid them in the soft warm loam
Of a dim shadowed place . . .
Deep
In a still cool grotto,
Lit only by the memories of stars

And the wide and luminous eyes
Of dead poets
That love me and that I love . . .
Deep . . . deep . . .
Where none may see—not even ye who gave—
About my soul your garden beautiful.

Under-Song

There is music in the strong
    Deep-throated bush,
Whisperings of song
    Heard in the leaves' hush—
Ballads of the trees
    In tongues unknown—
A reminiscent tone
    On minor keys . . .

Boughs swaying to and fro
    Though no winds pass . . .
Faint odors in the grass
    Where no flowers grow,
And flutterings of wings
    And faint first notes,
Once babbled on the boughs
    Of faded springs.

Is it music from the graves
    Of all things fair
Trembling on the staves
    Of spacious air—
Fluted by the winds
    Songs with no words—
Sonatas from the throats
    Of master birds?

One peering through the husk
    Of darkness thrown
May hear it in the dusk—
    That ancient tone,
Silvery as the light
    Of long dead stars
Yet falling through the night
    In trembling bars.

A Worn Rose

Where to-day would a dainty buyer
Imbibe your scented juice,
Pale ruin with a heart of fire;
Drain your succulence with her lips,
Grown sapless from much use . . .
Make minister of her desire
A chalice cup where no bee sips—
    Where no wasp wanders in?

Close to her white flesh housed an hour,
    One held you . . . her spent form
Drew on yours for its wasted dower—
What favor could she do you more?
    Yet, of all who drink therein,
    None know it is the warm
Odorous heart of a ravished flower
Tingles so in her mouth's red core . . .

The ore in the crucible is pungent, smelling like acrid wine,
It is dusky red, like the ebb of poppies,
And purple, like the blood of elderberries.
Surely it is a strong wine—juice distilled of the fierce iron.
I am drunk of its fumes.
I feel its fiery flux
Diffusing, permeating,
Working some strange alchemy . . .
So that I turn aside from the goodly board,
So that I look askance upon the common cup,[1]
And from the mouths of crucibles
Suck forth the acrid sap.

1. Taken together, the board and cup allude to the bread and wine of the Eucharist, which the speaker replaces with the acrid sap in the crucibles.

Dispossessed

Tender and tremulous green of leaves
Turned up by the wind,
Twanging among the vines—
Wind in the grass
Blowing a clear path
For the new-stripped soul to pass . . .

The naked soul in the sunlight . . .
Like a wisp of smoke in the sunlight
On the hill-side shimmering.

Dance light on the wind, little soul,[1]
Like a thistle-down floating
Over the butterflies
And the lumbering bees . . .

Come away from that tree

1. "Little soul": probably an allusion to the famous short poem composed by the Roman emperor Hadrian as a farewell to life (138 CE): "Little soul [animula], gentle, drifting, / Body's guest and partner, / In what place will you dwell now, / Pallid, rigid, naked, / No more to jest as you once did?" (My translation; for the Latin text, see Clark 2009.)

And its shadow grey as a stone . . .

Bathe in the pools of light
On the hillside shimmering—
Shining and wetted and warm in the sun-spray falling like golden
      rain—

But do not linger and look
At that bleak thing under the tree.

The Star

Last night
I watched a star fall like a great pearl into the sea,
Till my ego expanding encompassed sea and star,
Containing both as in a trembling cup.

(Easter 1916)

Censored lies that mimic truth . . .
    Censored truth as pale as fear . . .
My heart is like a rousing bell—
    And but the dead to hear . . .

My heart is like a mother bird,
    Circling ever higher,
And the nest-tree rimmed about
    By a forest fire . . .

My heart is like a lover foiled
    By a broken stair—
They are fighting to-night in Sackville Street,[1]
    And I am not there!

1. Now O'Connell Street, in Dublin; bombarded by the British during the Easter Rising of 1916, a short-lived armed rebellion by Irish Republicans against British rule. The event quickly became iconic. William Butler Yeats commemorated it in his famous poem "Easter, 1916." Sackville Street was the site of the General Post Office, which served as the rebellion's headquarters. (The building is still there.)

Appendix

The New Republic Version of "The Ghetto"

FIGURE 8. Outdoor market (Rivington Street), 1909. Wikimedia Commons.

Readers of the April 1918 issue of *The New Republic* would not have known that the poem published under the title "The Ghetto" was a selection of passages from a larger work; the poem was presented as a finished whole. It thus makes sense to regard the two texts as shorter and longer versions, each with its own distinctive features. The shorter version is reprinted below, with annotations to mark the few places in which its language differs from that of the longer version. The differences between the two begin with typography. The shorter version is freer with em-dashes and ellipses than the longer, and it thus has a more sporadic, more fragmentary texture. More important, the two versions differ in their large-scale form and its thematic implications.

Both versions begin with a description of Hester Street that develops into an account of the Sodos family, especially of Sadie, with whose character and love life segment I concludes. The shorter version then jumps immediately into the hurly-burly of commerce on the Ghetto streets (segment II). From there it returns without transition to the Sodos's tenement, recording the narrator's impression of the place, progressing through her observation of an old woman on a fire escape on Friday (Sabbath) evenings, and concluding with a wide-ranging erotic fantasia (segment III). In context this fantasia forms an elaboration of the earlier description of Sadie's sexuality. The segment ends with a metaphor in which Hester Street becomes a woman who awakens wearily to face another day of life in the Ghetto.

This cyclical form, with its implication of a governing order, is only vestigially present in the longer version of "The Ghetto." The greater length and breadth of the latter aim forwards—"Vorwärts"—at the breakthrough to Life, capital *L*, the transformation of raw energy into prolific vitality, that the shorter version does not find and perhaps does not seek.

The Ghetto

I

Cool, inaccessible air is floating in velvety blackness shot
    with steel-blue lights,
But no breath stirs the heat
Leaning its ponderous bulk upon the Ghetto
And most on Hester street . . . . .

The heat . . . . .
Nosing in the body's overflow,
Like a beast pressing its great steaming belly close,
Covering all avenues of air—
The heat in Hester street,
Heaped like a dray
With the garbage of the world.

I room at Sodos' with Sadie and her old father and her
mother—who is not so old and wears her own hair.[1]

Old Sodos no longer makes saddles.
He has forgotten how . . . . .
He has forgotten most things—even Bennie who stays away
    and sends wine on holidays—

1. This sentence is printed (with a phrase added) as four lines in the longer version.

And he does not like Sadie's mother
Who hides God's candles,
Nor Sadie
Whose young pagan breath puts out the light—
That should burn always,
Like Aaron's before the Lord.

Time spins like a crazy dial in his brain,
And night by night
I see the love-gesture of his arm
In its green-greasy coat-sleeve
Circling the Book,
And the candles gleaming starkly
On the blotched-paper whiteness of his face—
Like a mis-written psalm . . . . .
Night by night
I hear his lifted praise,
Like a broken whinnying
Before the Lord's shut gate.
Sadie dresses in black.
She has black-wet hair full of cold lights
And a fine-drawn face, too white.
All day the power machines
Drone in her ears . . . . .
All day the fine dust flies
Till throats are parched and itch
And the heat—like a kept corpse—
Fouls to the last corner.
Then—when needles move more slowly on the cloth
And sweaty fingers slacken
And hair falls in damp wisps over the eyes—
Sped by some power within,
Sadie quivers like a rod . . . . .

A thin black piston flying . . . . .
One with her machine.

She—who stabs the piece-work with her bitter eye
And bids the girls: "Slow down—
You'll have him cutting us again!
She—fiery static atom,
Held in place by the fierce pressure all about—
Speeds up the driven wheels
And biting steel—that twice
Has nipped her to the bone.

Nights, she reads
Those books that have most un-set thought,
New-poured and malleable,
To which her thought
Leaps fusing at white heat,
Or spits her fire out in some dim manger of a hall,
Or at a protest meeting on the Square . . . . .
Her lit eyes kindling the mob . . .
Or dances madly at a festival.
Each dawn finds her a little whiter,
Though up and keyed to the long day,
Alert, yet weary . . . . . like a bird
That all night long has beat about a light.

The Gentile lover, that she charms and shrews,
Is one more pebble in the pack
For Sadie's mother,
Who greets him with her narrowed eyes
That hold some welcome back.
"What's to be done?" she'll say,
"When Sadie wants she takes . . . . .

Better than Bennie with his Christian woman . . . . . .
A man is not so like,
If they should fight,
To call her Jew . . . . ."

Yet when she lies in bed
And the soft babble of their talk comes to her
And the silences . . . . . .
I know she never sleeps
Till the keen draught blowing up the empty hall
Edges through her transom
And she hears his foot on the first stairs.

II
Calicoes and furs,
Pocket-books and scarfs,
Razor strops and knives
(Patterns in check . . . . .)

Olive hands and russet head,
Pickles red and coppery,
Green pickles, brown pickles,
(Patterns in tapestry . . . . .)

Coral beads, blue beads,
Beads of pearl and amber,
Gewgaws, beauty pins—
Bijoutry for chits—
Darting rays of violet,
Amethyst and jade . . . . .
All the colors out to play,
Jumbled iridescently . . . . .
(Patterns in stained glass

Shivered into bits!)

Nooses of gay ribbon
Tugging at one's sleeve,
Dainty little garters
Hanging out their sign . . . . .
Here a pout of frilly things—
There a sonsy feather . . . . .
(White beards, black beards
Like knots in the weave . . . . .)

And ah, the little babies—
Shiny black-eyed babies—
(Half a million pink toes
Wriggling altogether.)
Baskets full of babies
Like grapes on a vine.

Mothers waddling in and out,
Making all things right—
Picking up the slipped threads
In Grand street at night—
Grand street like a great bazaar,
Crowded like a float,
Bulging like a crazy quilt
Stretched on a line.

But nearer seen
This litter of the East
Takes on a garbled majesty.
The herded stalls
In dissolute array . . . . .
The glitter and the jumbled finery

And strangely juxtaposed
Cans, paper, rags
And colors decomposing,
Faded like old hair,
With flashes of barbaric hues
And eyes of mystery . . . . .
Flung
Like an ancient tapestry of motley weave
Upon the open wall of this new land.

Here, a tawny-headed girl . . . . .
Lemons in a greenish broth
And a huge earthen bowl
By a bronzed merchant
With a tall black lamb's wool cap upon his head . . . . .
He has no glance for her.
His thrifty eyes
Bend—glittering, intent
Their hoarded looks
Upon his merchandise,
As though it were some splendid cloth
Or sumptuous raiment
Stitched in gold and red . . . . .
He seldom talks
Save of the goods he spreads—
The meager cotton with its dismal flower—
But with his skinny hands
That hover like two hawks
Above some luscious meat,
He fingers lovingly each calico,
As though it were a gorgeous shawl,
Or costly vesture
Wrought in silken thread,

Or strange bright carpet
Made for sandaled feet . . . . .

Here an old grey scholar stands.
His brooding eyes—
That hold long vistas without end
Of caravans and trees and roads,
And cities dwindling in remembrance—
Bend mostly on his tapes and thread.
What if they tweak his beard—
These raw young seed of Israel
Who have no backward vision in their eyes—
And mock him as he sways
Above the sunken arches of his feet—
They find no peg to hang their taunts upon.
His soul is like a rock
That bears a front worn smooth
By the coarse friction of the sea,
And, unperturbed, he keeps his bitter peace.

What if a rigid arm and stuffed blue shape,
Backed by a nickel star
Does prod him on,
Taking his proud patience for humility . . . . .
All gutters are as one
To that old race that has been thrust
From off the curbstones of the world . . . . .
And he smiles with the pale irony
Of one who holds
The wisdom of the Talmud stored away
In his mind's lavender.

Here this young trader—

Born to trade as to a caul—
Peddles the notions of the hour.
The gestures of the craft are his
And all the lore . . . . .
As when to hold, withdraw, persuade, advance . . . . .
And be it gum or flags,
Or clean-all or the newest thing in tags,
Demand goes to him as the bee to flower.
And he—appraising
All who come and go
With his amazing
Slight²-of-mind and glance
And nimble thought
And nature balanced like the scales at nought—
Looks Westward where the trade-lights glow,
And sees his vision rise—
A tape-ruled vision,
Circumscribed in stone—
Some fifty stories to the skies.

III.
As I sit in my little fifth-floor room
Bare,
Save for bed and chair,
And coppery stains
Left by seeping rains
On the low ceiling
And green plaster walls,
Where when night falls
Golden lady-bugs
Come out of their holes,

2. "Slight": corrected to "Sleight" in the longer version.

And roaches, sepia-brown, consort . . . . .
I hear bells pealing
Out of the gray church at Rutgers Street,
Holding its high-flung cross above the Ghetto,
And—one floor down across the court—
The parrot screaming:
Vorwärts . . . . . Vorwärts . . . . .
The parrot frowsy-white,
Everlastingly swinging
On its iron bar.

A little old woman,
With a wig of smooth black hair
Gummed about her shrunken brows,
Comes sometimes on the fire escape.
An old stooped mother—
The left shoulder low
With that uneven droopiness that women know
Who have suckled many young . . . . .
Yet I have seen no other than the parrot there.

I watch her mornings as she shakes her rugs
Feebly, with futile reach
And fingers without clutch.
Her thews are slack
And curved the ruined back
And flesh empurpled like old meat,
Yet each conspires
To feed those guttering fires
With which her eyes are quick.

On Friday nights
Her candles signal

Infinite fine rays
To other windows,
Coupling other lights . . . . .
Linking the tenements
Like an endless prayer.

She seems less lonely than the bird
That day by day about the dismal house
Screams out his frenzied word . . . . .
That night by night—
If a dog yelps
Or a cat yawls
Or a sick child whines,
Or a door screaks on its hinges,
Or a man and woman fight—
Sends his cry above the huddled roofs:
Vorwärts . . . . . Vorwärts . . . . .

Lights go out
And the stark trunks of the factories
Melt into the drawn darkness,
Sheathing like a seamless garment.

And mothers take home their babies,
Waxen and delicately curled,
Like little potted flowers closed under the stars.

The young men shut their eyes,[3]
But life turns in them . . . . .
Life in the cramped ova
Tearing and rending asunder its living cells . . . . .

3. In the longer version this line is preceded by the refrain, "Lights go out."

Trouble in unborn aeons . . . .
Wars, arts, discoveries, rebellions, travails, immolations,
        cataclysms, hates . . . . .
Pent in the shut flesh.

And the young men twist on their beds in languor and dizziness
        unsupportable . . . . .
Their eyes—heavy and dimmed
With dust of long oblivions in the gray pulp behind—
Staring as through a choked glass.
And they gaze at the moon—throwing off a faint heat—
The moon, blond and burning, creeping to their cots
Softly, as on naked feet . . . . .
Lolling on the coverlet . . . . . like a woman offering her white body.
Nude glory of the moon!
That leaps like an athlete on the bosoms of the young girls stripped
        of their linens;
Stroking their breasts that are smooth and cool as mother-of-pearl
Till the nipples tingle and burn as though little lips plucked at them.
They shudder and grow faint.
And their ears are filled as with a delirious rhapsody,
That Life, like a drunken player,
Strikes out of their clear white bodies
As out of ivory keys.

Lights go out . . .
And the great lovers linger in little groups, still passion-
        ately debating,
Or one may walk in silence, listening only to the still summons of
        Life—
Life making the great Demand . . . . .
Speaking in that loud, portentous voice . . . . .[4]

4. This line does not appear in the longer version.

Calling its new Christs . . .
Till tears come, blurring the stars that grow tender and comforting like
    the eyes of comrades;
And the moon rolls behind the Battery
Like a word molten out of the mouth of God.

Lights go out . . .
And colors rush together,
Fusing and floating away . . .
Pale worn gold like the settings of old jewels . . .
Mauves, exquisite, tremulous, and luminous purples
And burning spires in aureoles of light
Like shimmering auras.

They are covering up the pushcarts . . . . .
Now all have gone save an old man with mirrors—
Little oval mirrors like tiny pools.
He shuffles up a darkened street
And the moon burnishes his mirrors till they shine like phosphorus . . .
    . .
The moon like a skull,
Staring out of eyeless sockets at the old men trundling home the
    pushcarts.

A sallow dawn is in the sky
As I enter my little green room.

Sadie's light is still burning . . .

Without, the frail moon
Worn to a silvery tissue,
Throws a faint glamour on the roofs,
And down the shadowy spires

Lights tip-toe out . . .
Softly as when lovers close street doors.

Out of the Battery
A little wind
Stirs idly—as an arm
Trails over a boat's side in dalliance—
Rippling the smooth dead surface of the heat,
And Hester street,
Like a forlorn woman over-born
By many babies at her teats,
Turns on her trampled bed to meet the day.

References

Berke, Nancy. 2010. "'Electric Currents of Life': Lola Ridge's Immigrant *Flaneuserie*." *American Studies* 51: 27–47.

Carroll, Rory. 2016. "The Mysterious Lynching of Frank Little." *The Guardian*, September 21. www.theguardian.com/us-news/2016/sep/21/mysterious-lynching-of-frank-little-equality-activist. Accessed March 6, 2021.

Chatteron-Hill, Georges. 1914. *The Philosophy of Nietzsche*. London: Heath, Cranton, and Ouseley.

Clark, Tom. 2009. "Anima, Vagula, Blandula." *Beyond the Pale*, March 21. http://tomclarkblog.blogspot.com/2009/03/animula-vagula-blandula.html.

Crane, Hart. 2011. *The Bridge*. Edited and annotated by Lawrence Kramer. New York: Fordham University Press.

———. 1965. *Complete Poems and Selected Letters and Prose*. Edited by Brom Weber. New York: Anchor Books.

Derby, Mark. 2009. "Ridge, Lola: Anarchist and Poet." libcom.org/history/lola-ridge-anarchist-poet.

Eliot, T. S. 1963. *Collected Poems, 1909–1962*. New York: Harcourt, Brace, and World.

Gates, Henry Louis, Jr. 1987. *Figures in Black: Words, Signs, and the "Racial" Self*. New York: Oxford University Press.

James, Henry. 1993. *Collected Travel Writings: Great Britain and America*. New York: Library of America.

Kaladjian, Walter, ed. 2015. *The Cambridge Companion to Modern American Poetry*. Cambridge: Cambridge University Press.

Kreymbourg, Alfred. 1919. "A Poet in Arms." *Poetry Magazine* 13 (March): 335–40.

Landmarks Preservation Commission. 1997. "Historic Street Lampposts." s-media.nyc.gov/agencies/lpc/lp/1961.pdf.

Leinenweber, Charles. 1977. "Socialists in the Streets." *Science and Society* 41: 152–71.

Marx, Karl. 2009. "On the Jewish Question." Translation unattributed. www.marxists.org/archive/marx/works/1844/jewish-question/index.htm.

Maun, Carolyn. 2012. *Mosaic of Fire: The Work of Lola Ridge, Evelyn Scott, Charlotte Wilder, and Kay Boyle.* Columbia: University of South Carolina Press.

Nevlus, James. 2017. "The Ever Changing Bowery." *Longform*, October 4. ny.curbed.com/2017/10/4/16413696/bowery-nyc-history-lower-east-side.

Pinsky, Robert. 2011. "Street Poet." *Slate*. www.slate.com/articles/arts/poem/2011/03/street_poet.html.

Rossetti, Christina. 1865. *Goblin Market and Other Poems.* Google Books. www.google.com/books/edition/Goblin_Market/tcUVAAAAYAAJ?hl=en.

Rumens, Carol. 2018. "Poem of the Week: 'Manhattan' by Lola Ridge." *The Guardian*, October 15. www.theguardian.com/books/booksblog/2018/oct/15/poem-of-the-week-manhattan-by-lola-ridge.

Scott, Bonnie Kime, ed. 2007. *Gender in Modernism: New Geographies, Complex Intersections.* Urbana: University of Illinois Press.

Shelley, Percy Bysshe. 1820. "Ode to the West Wind." https://en.wikisource.org/wiki/Prometheus_Unbound;_a_lyrical_drama_in_four_acts_with_other_poems/Ode_to_the_West_Wind.

Simonds, Sandra. 2020. "Lola Ridge / Morris Rosenfeld." *Sandra Simonds: Poet and Critic.* www.sandrasimondspoet.com/2020/02/25/lola-ridge-morris-rosenfeld/.

Svoboda, Terese. 2016a. *Anything that Burns You: A Portrait of Lola Ridge, Radical Poet.* Tucson, AZ: Schaffner Press.

———. 2016b. "Lola Ridge, a Great Irish Writer and Why You've Never Heard of Her." *Irish Times*, October 4. www.irishtimes.com/culture/books/lola-ridge-a-great-irish-writer-and-why-you-ve-never-heard-of-her-1.2816113.

Untermeyer, Louis. 1919. Review of *The Ghetto and Other Poems. New York Evening Post*, February 1. NYS Historic Newspapers. nyshistoricnewspapers.org/lccn/sn83030384/.

Whitman, Walt. 2002. *Leaves of Grass and Other Writings.* Edited by Michael Moon. New York: Norton Critical Editions.

Williams, William Carlos. 1917. *Al Que Quiere!* Boston: Four Seas. Google Books. www.google.com/books/edition/_/dtIEAQAAIAAJ?hl=en&gbpv=1.

Lola Ridge (1873, Dublin–1941, Brooklyn) was a poet and editor active in many radical causes and in avant-garde literary circles in New York in the decades before the world wars. She published five volumes of poetry between 1918 and 1935 and served as an editor at two leading modernist journals, *The Broom* and *Others*. Two (unannotated) collections of her early poetry have been published in recent years, edited by Daniel Tobin.

Lawrence Kramer is Distinguished Professor of English and Music at Fordham University. He is the author of fifteen books, as well as editor of two previous annotated editions of poetry: *Walt Whitman's Drum-Taps: The Complete 1865 Edition* (NYRB, 2015) and *Hart Crane's 'The Bridge': An Annotated Edition* (Fordham, 2011).